# How to Use

Macromedia®

# Flash™ MX and ActionScript

Denise Tyler

**que**®

201 W. 103rd Street
Indianapolis, Indiana 46290

# How to Use Macromedia® Flash™ MX and ActionScript

International Standard Book Number: 0-7897-2742-0

Library of Congress Catalog Card Number: 2001099407

Printed in the United States of America

First Printing: July 2002

05   04   03   02         4   3   2   1

## Trademarks

## Warning and Disclaimer

**Publisher**
David Culverwell

**Executive Editor**
Candace Hall

**Acquisitions Editor**
Kate Small

**Development Editor**
Damon Jordan

**Managing Editor**
Thomas F. Hayes

**Project Editor**
Tonya Simpson

**Production Editor**
Megan Wade

**Indexer**
Ken Johnson

**Proofreader**
Lisa Wilson

**Technical Editor**
Gary Rebholtz

**Team Coordinator**
Cindy Teeters

**Interior Designer**
Anne Jones

**Cover Designer**
Anne Jones

# Contents at a Glance

# Contents

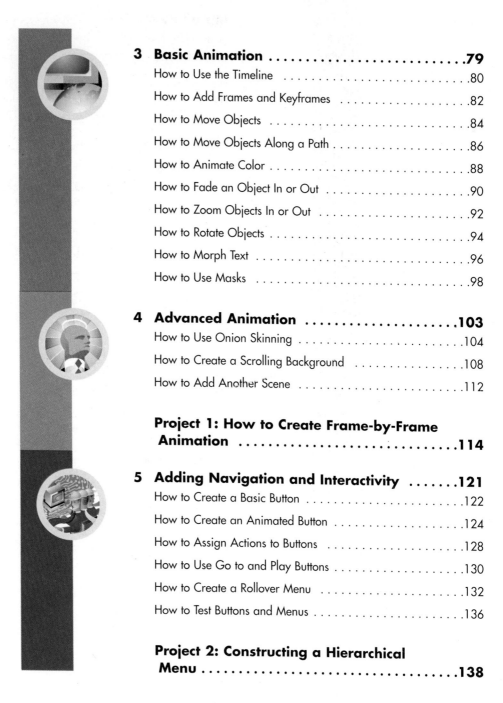

## About the Author

**Denise Tyler** is no stranger to graphics, animation, and multimedia-related software. During many years of working as a freelance graphics artist and animator, she attained wide and varied experience with many computer graphics, animation, and Web-related software programs, including Macromedia Flash. She was formerly a Consulting and Training Specialist for Sonic Foundry in Madison, Wisconsin, where she combined her passion for multimedia with an equal passion for teaching others how to create it.

An author for Pearson Education and Sams Publishing since 1994, Denise has authored, coauthored, or revised more than a dozen books relating to computer graphics and Web page development. Her projects include updates and revisions for Laura Lemay's international best-selling book, *Sams Teach Yourself Web Publishing with HTML 4 in 21 Days*. This is her first book for Que.

## Dedication

*To Mom and Dad—even though many miles separate us, you're always close to my heart. Love always, Denise.*

## Acknowledgements

If you look back a few pages in this book, you'll see a list of quite a few people who worked along with me on this book. Although many of these people are "names without a face," their contributions to this work are no less important than my own. In each book I write, I try to thank all those who were part of the team that helped put this book together. So, let me start by saying thanks to all the editors, indexers, proofreaders, coordinators, designers, and technicians who helped make this book. Special thanks go to Damon Jordan, Megan Wade, and Gary Rebholtz for their assistance with development, copy editing, and technical editing.

Most especially, I'd like to thank two of my long-time friends at Sams/Pearson Education for yet another opportunity to help people learn how to use cool software. These are two of the virtually busiest people on the planet, yet Jeff Schultz and Kate Small have been there for me through thick and thin...always cheery, always patient, and always with healthy senses of humor. In the many projects that we have worked on together, both have taken a place at the top of my list of dearest friends. Thanks, guys—you are truly special!

Denise Tyler

## We Want to Hear from You!

As the reader of this book, *you* are our most important critic and commentator. We value your opinion and want to know what we're doing right, what we could do better, what areas you'd like to see us publish in, and any other words of wisdom you're willing to pass our way.

As an executive editor for Que, I welcome your comments. You can email or write me directly to let me know what you did or didn't like about this book—as well as what we can do to make our books better.

Please note that I cannot help you with technical problems related to the *topic* of this book. We do have a User Services group, however, where I will forward specific technical questions related to the book.

When you write, please be sure to include this book's title and author as well as your name, email address, and phone number. I will carefully review your comments and share them with the author and editors who worked on the book.

Email:      feedback@quepublishing.com

Mail:       Candace Hall
            Que Publishing
            201 West 103rd Street
            Indianapolis, IN 46290 USA

For more information about this book or another Que title, visit our Web site at www.quepublishing.com. Type the ISBN (excluding hyphens) or the title of a book in the Search field to find the page you're looking for.

# The Complete Visual Reference

Each chapter of this book is made up of a series of short, instructional tasks designed to help you understand all the information that you need to get the most out of your computer hardware and software.

 **Click:** Click the left mouse button once.

 **Double-click:** Click the left mouse button twice in rapid succession.

 **Right-click:** Click the right mouse button once.

 **Drag:** Click and hold the left mouse button, position the mouse pointer, and release.

 **Pointer Arrow:** Highlights an item on the screen you need to point to or focus on in the step or task.

**Selection:** Highlights the area onscreen discussed in the step or task.

 **Type:** Click once where indicated and begin typing to enter your text or data.

 **Drag and Drop:** Point to the starting place or object. Hold down the mouse button (right or left per instructions), move the mouse to the new location, and then release the button.

Each task includes a series of easy-to-understand steps designed to guide you through the procedure.

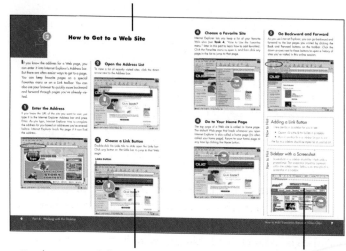

Each step is fully illustrated to show you how it looks onscreen.

Extra hints that tell you how to accomplish a goal are provided in most tasks.

Keyboard shortcuts are provided throughout the text. Macintosh shortcuts are listed first in parenthesis, such as (⌘-**E**). Windows shortcuts are listed second in brackets, such as **[Ctrl+E]**.

Menus and items you click and keyboard shortcuts are shown in **bold**. Words in *italic* are defined in more detail in the glossary. Information you type is in a `special font`.

# Introduction

There aren't many programs that are as fun and easy to use as Macromedia Flash. Flash helps you create stylish interfaces and animations that zip through your Internet pipeline at blazing speeds. Your Flash movies can be as simple as moving text or as complex as its robust ActiveScript will allow.

Macromedia Flash contains a suite of clever drawing and animation tools that are easy (and fun) to learn and use. If you find it difficult to draw with a mouse, have no fear. The best part about Flash's drawing tools is that they actually make drawing with a mouse much easier. If you want, you can configure Flash to smooth out those rough lines and automatically optimize your shapes so they are lean and mean and download quickly.

Animation is also a breeze with Flash. You can use tweens that automatically generate additional frames between a "start" frame and an "end" frame. Or, if you prefer, you can create traditional frame-by-frame animation with the help of Flash's onion-skin feature, which helps you view the content of surrounding frames while you manually draw the in-between frames. This book shows examples of both types of animation techniques and more.

## In This Book

Before you work your way through this book, we recommend that you complete the lessons Macromedia furnishes with the program. These lessons will help you become familiar with the Flash tools and Flash interface. To view and start the lessons, select Help, Lessons, and select the lesson you want to learn.

If you want to go beyond those lessons quickly, you don't want a lot of explanation or wordy introductions, and you don't want to bog yourself down with a lot of technical features and jargon. You just want to dig right in and learn. This is the book for you!

This book has a specific goal in mind: to teach you the basics of Flash in a systematic way that is easy to follow.

Although you learn how to create animations, the book won't tie you down with having to draw everything in each frame by hand. Instead, we'll show you how to reuse, modify, or "tween" objects so that Flash does most of the work for you.

This book won't bog you down with a lot of technical details and features, either. It teaches you enough of the basics to get you well on your way toward creating what Flash is best known for. Although much of Flash's power lies in using advanced scripting features, the steps to explain how to use them would fill another book at least this size. We will, however, show you some very basic scripting techniques that perform basic navigation functions and more.

This visual guide to Flash will get you started (if you'll pardon the pun) in a flash. Each step displays a picture that shows the process or result. By the time you complete this book, you'll know how to use Flash to accomplish the following tasks, plus a whole lot more:

- Paint and draw shapes using all the tools in the Flash toolbox
- Import artwork that you create in other software applications
- Use and organize layers in your Flash movies
- Create buttons that navigate to Web pages, other Flash movies, and other scenes in the same Flash movie
- Use keyframes, tweens, and onion-skinning to create animations
- Add sounds to your Flash movies
- Optimize and publish your Flash projects

Pull up your favorite chair to your monitor and keyboard, fire up the CPU, and turn the pages in this book to learn what Flash is about. You'll be up and running in no time!

# Introducing Macromedia Flash

If you're reading this book, you're probably already familiar with Macromedia Flash. Flash is used on innumerable Web sites to enhance content with rich, clean, sharp multimedia that downloads and streams quickly. When you selected Flash as the way to integrate multimedia into your Web sites, you made a wise choice. In spite of all its features, Flash is easy to use! You'll also enjoy hearing that you'll be up and running in no time with the help of the examples provided in this book.

As with any well-designed software program, Flash is easy to learn. After you're familiar with the lay of the land, you'll find the interface to be very intuitive—things make sense. In addition, Flash contains a depth that just keeps unfolding before you as you work with the program.

Every project begins with a first step. The tasks in this part of the book begin with a general overview of the Flash interface and continue by explaining where you can find the commands and features you need.

# Welcome to Macromedia Flash

This task walks you through opening and exiting Flash and familiarizes you with its basic interface, which features standard Windows commands, toolbars, and shortcuts. We'll also open one of the sample files that ships with Flash. Let's get started!

## 1 Open Macromedia Flash

To open Flash from the Windows XP start menu, select **Start**, **All Programs**, **Macromedia**, **Macromedia Flash MX**. To open Flash on your Mac, locate the folder that contains the Flash shortcut, and double-click the shortcut to open the program.

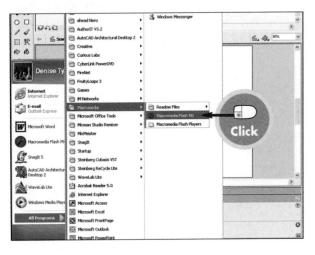

## 2 General Interface Layout

The toolbars located on the left side of the screen provide quick access to drawing tools and commands. The Timeline gives you a bird's-eye view of the layers and actions that take place in your movie. Use the Stage to develop and view the objects and symbols in your movie.

| Tools toolbar | Timeline | Zoom options |

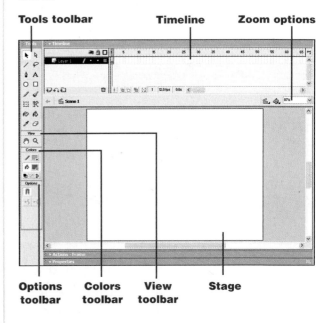

| Options toolbar | Colors toolbar | View toolbar | Stage |

### How to Hint

## The Toolbar (Windows Only)

Windows users can display or hide a toolbar that contains buttons for several commonly used commands. To display the toolbar, select **Window**, **Toolbars, Main**. The toolbar appears beneath the menu bar by default, but you can drag it to another position on the Stage.

## ③ The Properties Window

To show or hide the Properties window, select **Window**, **Properties** or use the shortcut (⌘-**F3**) [**Ctrl+F3**]. The Properties window appears below the Stage by default, but you can undock it and move it to a different location. Use this panel to configure options for the tool you have selected.

## ④ The Panels

Flash includes a number of additional panels that enable you to specify various settings for the elements on the Stage. The right portion of the screen displays several of these panels, most notably the Color Mixer and Color Swatches panels, which enable you to choose or create colors for your movies. Use commands in the Window menu to display or hide additional panels.

Color Swatches        Color Mixer

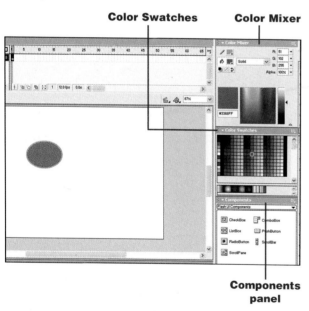

Components panel

## ⑤ The Timeline and Stage

When you develop your movies, you'll frequently use the Stage and Timeline. You place objects on the Stage to display them in your movie. Then, you add frames and keyframes in the Timeline to control the length and animation in your movie.

Timeline        Stage

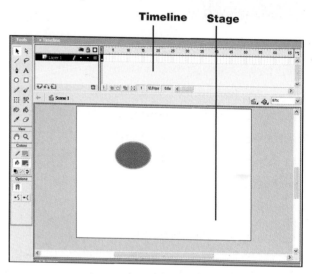

## ⑥ Exit Macromedia Flash MX

To exit Flash MX, select **File**, **Quit** (⌘-**Q**) on the Mac or **File**, **Exit** [**Ctrl+Q**] in Windows. If you have any unsaved changes, Flash MX prompts you to save them to your hard drive.

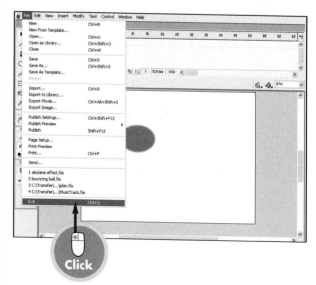

Click

# How to Use Macromedia Flash Tools

**A**lthough Flash provides many drawing tools, you basically use the same steps to use each of them. You select a tool from the Tools panel, select colors from the Colors panel, and set options for the tools in the Tools panel. This task gives you a quick overview of these steps.

## ① Select a Tool

Flash tools fall into three basic categories. Drawing tools (Line, Pen, Text, Oval, Rectangle, Pencil, and Brush) enable you to create lines, objects, and shapes. Selection tools (Arrow, Subselect, and Lasso) select items for modification or grouping, and modification tools enable you to modify shapes (Free Transform, Fill Transform, Ink Bottle, Paint Bucket, and Eyedropper).

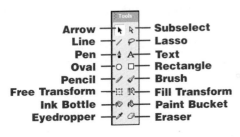

## ② Select a Color

If you select one of the drawing tools, the next step is to select a color. The Colors panel provides a quick way to select stroke colors (represented by the pencil) and fill colors (represented by the paint bucket). Simply click either color square to select from a palette of Web-safe colors.

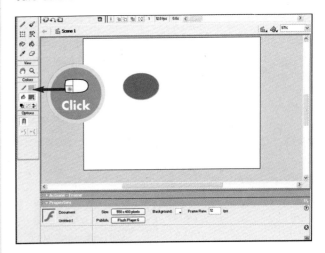

---

How to Hint

## Switching Tools

When you switch tools, Flash retains the stroke and fill colors you last used.

## ③ Additional Color Options

If you want to choose or create a custom color, use the **Color Mixer** to specify a color by Red, Green, and Blue values (RGB); Hue, Saturation, and Brightness values (HSB); or Hexadecimal values (such as FFCC00). Use the **Add Swatch** command in the Color Mixer options menu to save your color to the Color Swatches palette if desired.

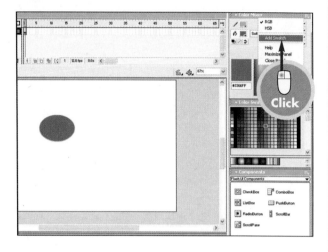

## ④ Choose Tool Options

The Arrow, Lasso, Rectangle, Pencil, Brush, Free Transform, Paint Bucket, and Eraser tools offer options that determine how each tool will be used. Select the options from the **Options** panel before you use the selected tool. For example, the Pencil tool offers three drawing styles: Straight, Smooth, and Ink.

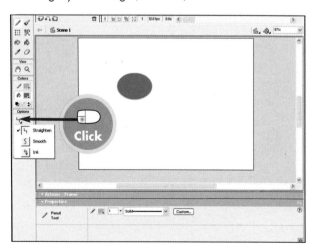

## ⑤ Additional Tool Options

Additional options for the selected tool might appear in the Properties window, which appears below the Stage by default. If the Properties window is not open, select **Window**, **Properties** to display it. In the example shown, the Properties window allows you to customize the width and type of stroke that the pencil draws.

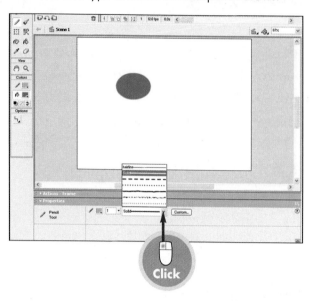

## ⑥ Go to the Stage

Now that you have selected the tool and its options, go to the Stage and use the drawing tools to draw a shape, or use the selection tools to select the objects you want to work on.

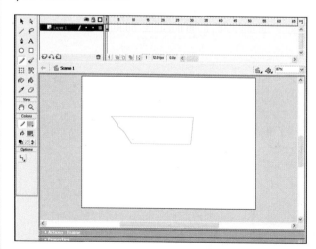

# How to Use Macromedia Flash Panels

Flash provides a number of panels that enable you to manipulate the objects on your Stage. This task gives you an overview of some of the most commonly used panels.

## ❶ Size and Move Objects Precisely

The Properties window and the Info panel (⌘-**I**) [**Ctrl+I**] display size and coordinate information you can edit to resize or move the selected object. To resize an object, enter new values in the **W** and **H** fields. To move the object, enter new values in the **X** (horizontal) or **Y** (vertical) field.

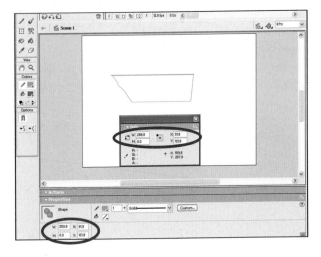

## ❷ Align, Distribute, and Match Objects

Select **Window**, **Align** or press (⌘-**K**) [**Ctrl+K**] to open the Align panel. This panel helps you align multiple selected objects, distribute them evenly, and match size and spacing. Simply click a button to perform the desired operation.

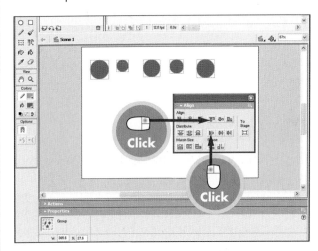

---

## How to Hint

### Advanced Panels

Flash also provides additional panels for advanced features, such as scripting. Included among the advanced panels are the Actions panel (which assigns actions to frames and buttons), the Debugger (which helps you debug your scripting), and the Reference panel (which contains command and property references). You will work with the Actions panel later in this book.

## ③ Scale, Rotate, and Skew Objects Precisely

In addition to the Free Transform tool located in the Tools panel, you can use the Transform Panel (⌘-T) [**Ctrl+T**] to scale, rotate, or skew an object. You can precisely scale the width and height, rotation, or skewing by entering numerical values. A button in the lower-right corner of the panel applies the transform to a copy of the object and leaves the original untouched.

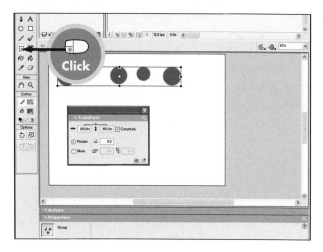

## ④ Play Your Movies

Select **Window**, **Toolbars**, **Controller** to display the Controller panel. This panel enables you to start and stop your movie, as well as navigate to the previous or next frame or to the start or end of the movie using VCR-like controls. The controls are disabled if the movie contains only one frame.

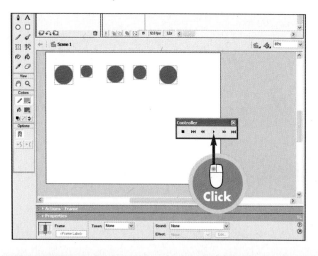

## ⑤ Store and Use Symbols

Select **Window**, **Library** or use the shortcut **F11** to display the project library. The library enables you to store and organize all the symbols in your movies. You can also use symbols from other libraries in any Flash project.

## ⑥ Customize the Panel Layout

If you find that you use some panels more than others, you can save a custom layout. After you arrange the panels the way you want them to appear onscreen, select **Window**, **Save Panel Layout**. Assign a name to the layout and click **OK**. Flash then saves the panel layout to your hard drive. To load the custom layout, select **Window**, **Panel Sets**, and then select a layout from the flyout menu.

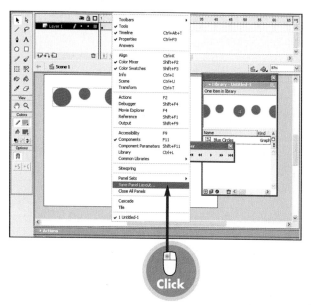

# How to Create and Configure a New Movie

**E**very Flash project you create is called a *movie*. When you create a movie, you specify the dimensions of the movie and the speed of the movie in frames per second (fps). The background color of the movie determines the color of the Web page on which it appears after you publish the movie. You can also specify the spacing and color of the grid that lines and objects snap to.

## ❶ Select the File, New Command

Flash starts a new movie every time you open the application. To create a new movie at any other time, either select **File**, **New** or use the keyboard shortcut (⌘**-N**) [**Ctrl+N**]. Windows users can also use the **New** button on the toolbar.

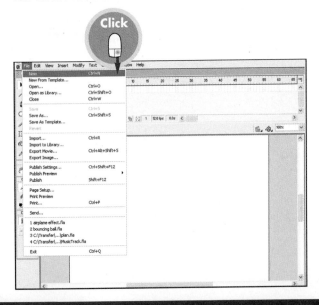

## ❷ Set the Movie Size

Select **Modify**, **Document** to display the Document Properties dialog box. To change the movie size, click the **Size** button. In the Document Properties dialog box, enter **Width** and **Height** values between 18 and 2880.

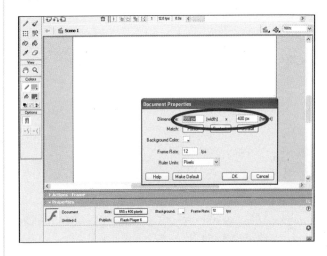

## How to Hint

### Customizing Movie Background Colors

If you need to use a color that is not in the default palette, you can use the Color Mixer (**Shift+F9**) to create custom background colors for your movie. After you click the Background Color square in the Properties window, you can drag an eyedropper to the Color Mixer and click to select a color.

## ③ Choose the Background Color

To modify the color of the movie background, click the **Background Color** square in the Properties window or Document Properties dialog box. Then, select a color from your current color palette. Click **OK** to exit the dialog box. The background of the movie changes to the selected color.

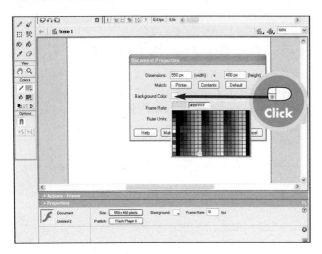

## ⑤ Choose the Macromedia Flash Version

By default, Flash MX publishes movies that are compatible with Flash Player 6. You can also publish movies that are compatible with earlier versions. Click the **Publish** button in the Properties window to open the Publish Settings dialog box, and select an earlier version from the **Version** drop-down list.

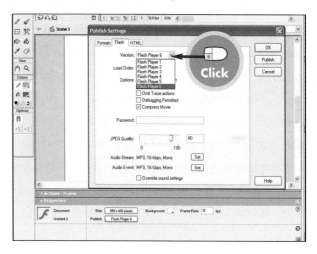

## ④ Set the Frame Rate

To set the frame rate for the movie, enter the number of frames per second in the **Frame Rate** field, which appears in either the Properties window or the Document Properties dialog box. Web animations typically use frame rates of 8fps–12fps, with 12fps as the default setting.

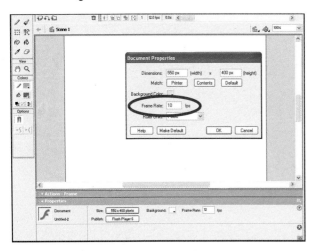

## ⑥ Name Your Movie

To name and save your movie, select **File**, **Save** or use the shortcut (⌘-**S**) [**Ctrl+S**]. From the Save As dialog box, navigate to the folder into which you want to save the file. Enter a name in the **File Name** field, and click **Save** to save the file to the selected folder.

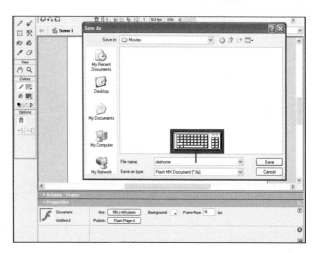

# How to Use Macromedia Flash Drawing Aids

**B**efore you start drawing your objects on the Stage, you might want to enable and configure some of Flash's drawing aids, which help you draw and arrange your shapes and objects more easily. Rulers, grids, and snapping help you size and position objects accurately, whereas drawing preferences help you draw with a mouse more easily. You'll learn about these features in the following steps.

## ① Configure the Grid

Select **View**, **Grid**, **Edit Grid.** In the Grid dialog box, click the **Color** square to select a grid color. Enter a grid size, in pixels, in the horizontal and vertical spacing fields. Select a snap accuracy option from the drop-down list and click the **Save Default** button to save the new default settings, if desired.

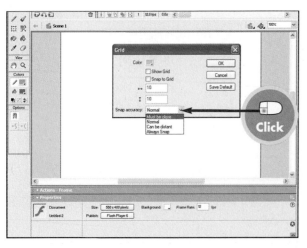

## ② Display the Grid

To display the grid on the Stage, either check the **Show Grid** option in the Grid dialog box (shown in step 3) or select **View**, **Grid**, **Show Grid** to toggle the feature on. Uncheck the option or repeat the command to hide the grid.

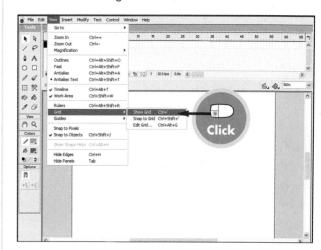

## ③ Snap to the Grid

When you enable the Snap to Grid option, all shapes and lines snap to grid points, whether the grid is displayed. To enable grid snapping, check the **Snap to Grid** option in the Grid dialog box (shown in step 3) or select **View**, **Grid**, **Snap to Grid**.

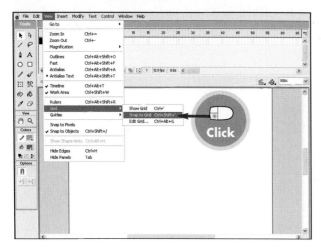

## ④ Display the Rulers

You can display the rulers to help you draw guides on the Stage. Select **View**, **Rulers** to display rulers along the top and left edges of the Stage.

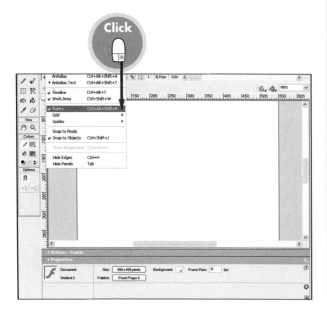

## ⑤ Change the Ruler Units

The ruler displays units in pixels by default. To change the ruler units, select **Modify**, **Document** to open the Document Properties dialog box. Then, select **Inches**, **Inches (decimal)**, **Points**, **Centimeters**, **Millimeters**, or **Pixels** from the **Ruler Units** drop-down list.

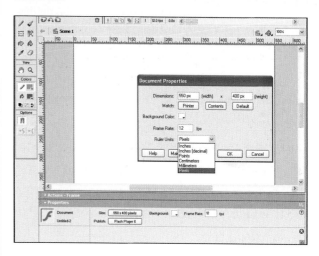

## ⑥ Create One or More Guides

To create a horizontal guide using the ruler, click and drag from the top ruler onto the Stage. A guide line follows the cursor. Release the mouse button to set the guide into position. Similarly, to create a vertical guide, click and drag from the left ruler onto the Stage and release to set the guide position.

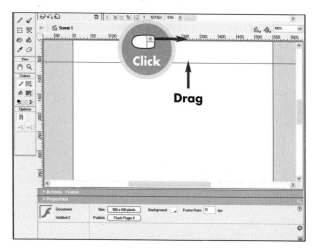

## (7) Change the Guide Color and Snap Accuracy

You can edit the color and snap accuracy of the guides. To do so, select **View**, **Guides**, **Edit Guides** to open the Guides dialog box. Click the **Color** square to select a new guide color from the current palette. Then, select an option from the **Snap Accuracy** drop-down list (Must **Be Close**, **Normal**, or **Can Be Distant**).

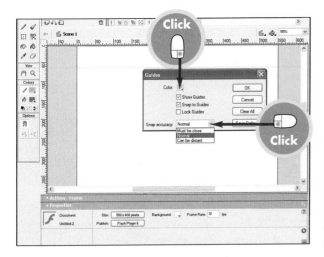

### Clearing Guides from the Stage

To clear the guides from the Stage, select **View**, **Guides**, **Edit Guides** to open the Guides dialog box. Click the **Clear All** button, and then click **OK** to exit the dialog box.

## (8) Lock and Snap to the Guides

You can lock the guides in place so that you do not move them inadvertently. To lock the guides, select **View**, **Guides**, **Lock Guides** or check the **Lock Guides** option in the Guides dialog box (shown in step 7). To enable the Snap to Guides feature, select **View**, **Guides**, **Snap to Guides** or check the **Snap to Guides** option in the Guides dialog box.

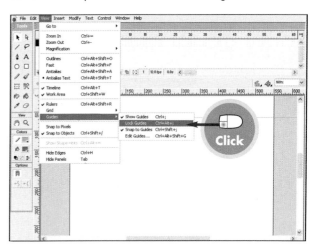

## (9) Set Drawing Preferences

Select **Edit**, **Preferences** to open the Preferences dialog box; then click the **Editing** tab. Several options in the **Drawing Settings** section make drawing with a mouse in Flash much easier.

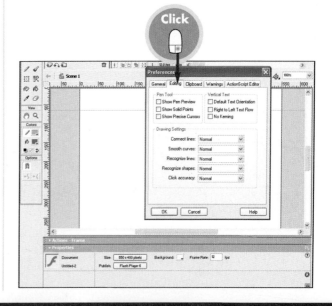

## ⑩ Connect Lines Automatically

The Connect Lines setting controls how far apart two lines should be before Flash MX automatically snaps their ends together for you. Select **Must Be Close**, **Normal** (default), or **Can Be Distant**.

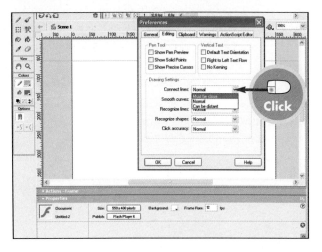

## ⑪ Automatically Smooth Curves

Flash can also smooth freehand lines for you automatically. The Smooth Curves drop-down list enables you to choose the amount of smoothness that will be applied. Options are Off (no smoothing), Rough (a small amount of smoothing), Normal, and Smooth (maximum amount of smoothing).

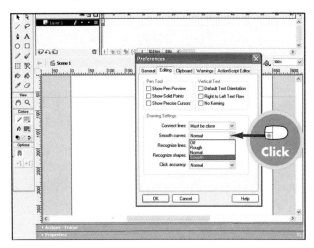

## ⑫ Control Line and Shape Recognition

The Recognize Lines and Recognize Shapes settings control how straight lines must be and how close shapes are to true geometric shapes before Flash recognizes them. Options for both types of recognition are Off (no recognition), Strict (lines and shapes must be near-perfect), Normal, and Tolerant (lines and shapes can be less perfect).

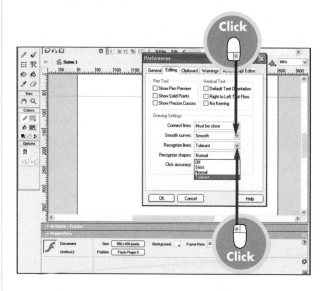

## ⑬ Set the Click Accuracy

The Click Accuracy setting determines how close an item must be to the mouse pointer before Flash recognizes the item. Options are Strict (very close), Normal, and Tolerant (not as close).

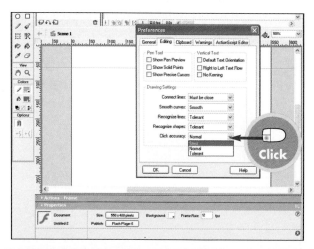

# How to Create and Group Shapes and Strokes

The Oval and Rectangle tools are frequently used to create basic shapes such as ovals, circles, rectangles, and squares. These basic shapes are the building blocks for navigation buttons, menu backgrounds, text backgrounds, and other decorative shapes. You can configure the tool to create a shape without an outline or an outline without a fill if you desire. Settings in the Properties window also enable you to customize the appearance of the outline.

## 1 Create Ovals and Rectangles

The Oval and Rectangle tools are great for creating basic button shapes, and the steps to use them are very similar. Begin by selecting either the **Oval** or **Rectangle** tool.

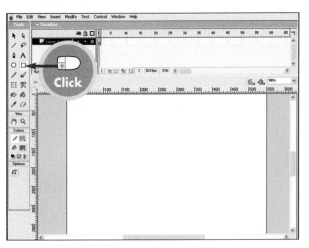

## 2 Choose Stroke and Fill Colors

From the Colors palette, or from the Properties window, select a stroke color (pencil icon) and a fill color (paint bucket icon) from the current palette.

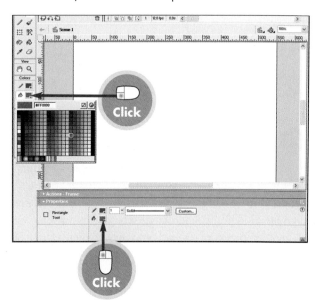

## ③ Turn Off Stroke or Fill Color

If you want to create a filled rectangle without a stroke or a stroked rectangle without a fill, select the color you want to turn off (either the outline color or the fill color). Then, click the **No Color** option in the Colors panel.

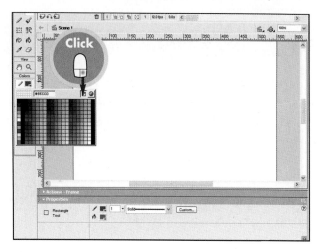

## ④ Specify Stroke Size

If your shape has a stroke, use the **Stroke Height** field in the Properties window to enter the thickness in pixels. Alternatively, click the arrow at the right of the field to adjust the stroke height with a slider. Move the slider up to increase the value or down to decrease the value.

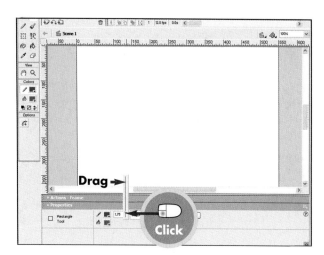

## ⑤ Specify Stroke Style

Select an option from the **Stroke Style** drop-down list. You can choose from a selection of solid, dashed, dotted, or broken lines. Click to select the desired stroke style. Please note, however, that the more complicated stroke styles make the movie less lean.

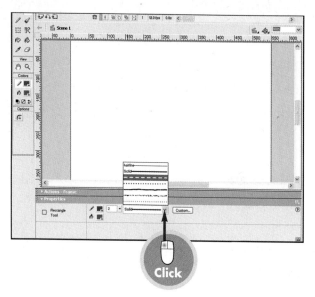

## ⑥ Create a Custom Stroke Style

To create a custom stroke style, click the **Custom** button to open the Stroke Style dialog box. Select a stroke style (Solid, Dashed, Dotted, Ragged, Stipple, or Hatched). Then, select additional appearance options that appear. A preview of your stroke appears in the dialog box.

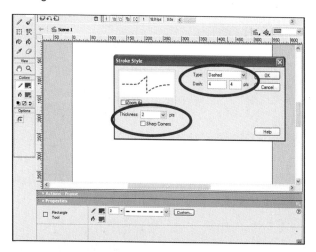

### ⑦ Use the Custom Stroke

Click **OK** to exit the Stroke Style dialog box. The custom stroke then appears in the Stroke Style drop-down list and selects it automatically.

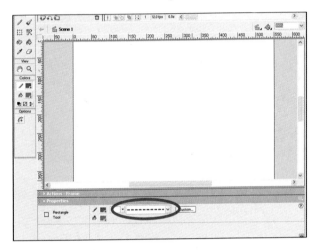

### ⑧ Draw the Shape

Click the Stage to set the upper-left corner of the shape. Drag toward the bottom-right corner and release the mouse to create the shape.

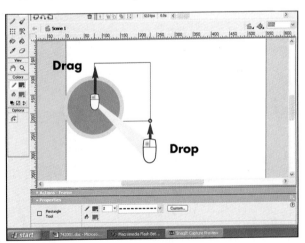

### ⑨ Create Circles and Squares

To constrain the Oval or Rectangle tool so that you create a perfect circle or square, Shift-click and drag from the upper-left corner to the bottom-right corner. Release the mouse button; then release the Shift key to create the shape.

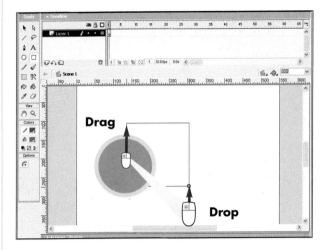

### ⑩ Create Rounded Rectangles

To create a rounded rectangle, select the **Rectangle** tool. Click the **Round Rectangle Radius** button in the Options panel to open the Rectangle Settings dialog box.

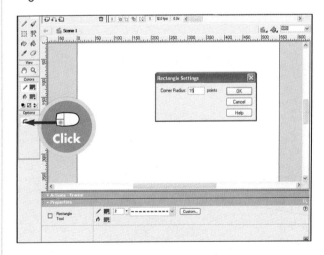

## 11 Set the Corner Radius and Draw

In the **Corner Radius** field, enter the number of points at which to size the corner radius. For example, enter **15** points, as shown here. Next, click **OK** to exit the dialog box, and draw the rectangle in the usual manner.

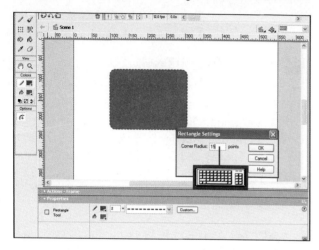

## 12 Select the Ungrouped Shape

If your shape consists of an outline and a fill, each item is actually a separate object. Shift-click to select the outline and then the fill, or double-click the fill with the Arrow tool to select both the outline and the fill.

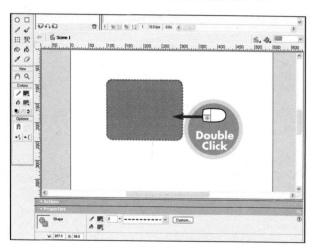

## 13 Group the Shape

To group the line or fill as a single object, select **Modify**, **Group** (⌘-**G**) [**Ctrl+G**].

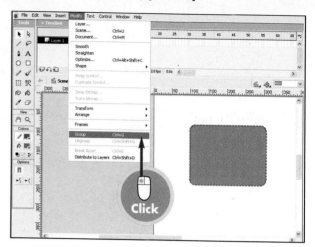

### How to Hint

## Reshaping Before You Group

You'll learn in Task 8, "How to Edit and Reshape Lines," how to reshape lines and fills. Experiment with this feature to create even more interesting button and menu shapes. Reshaping the buttons before you group the outline and fill together is easiest.

# How to Draw Lines

Flash offers a host of other tools that enable you to draw lines, shapes, and fills. These tools work with either a line color or a fill color, but not both.

## 1 Draw Straight Lines

The Line tool uses the Stroke color to draw straight or diagonal lines. After you select the Line tool, use the Properties window to select the stroke color, stroke height, and stroke style. Click to set the start of the line. Keep the left mouse button pressed while you drag to a new position, and release the mouse button to set the end of the line.

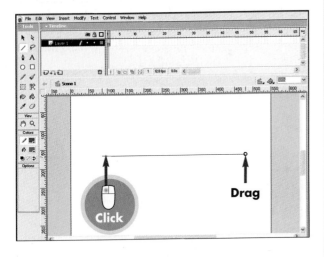

## 2 The Pencil Tool

The Pencil tool enables you to draw freehand straight or curved lines, and it uses the Stroke color. Select the color, stroke height, and stroke style from the Properties panel, as described earlier in Task 6, "How to Create and Group Shapes and Strokes."

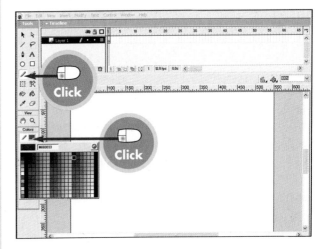

### ③ Choose a Pencil Mode

When you select the Pencil tool, the Options panel displays the Pencil Mode icon. The mode you select determines the appearance of your pencil strokes.

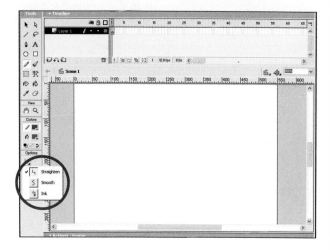

### ④ Use Straighten Mode

Select **Straighten** to straighten your strokes as much as possible. When you draw your strokes, draw them as straight as you can and as close to the shape as you want to draw (such as a square, rectangle, or triangle). When you release the mouse, Flash straightens the lines as close to the angle that you originally drew.

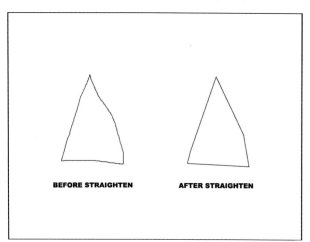

### ⑤ Use Smooth Mode

Select **Smooth** to smooth out the rough edges in the strokes you draw. If your line is slightly jaggy, Flash smoothes it out and reduces the number of segments in the lines.

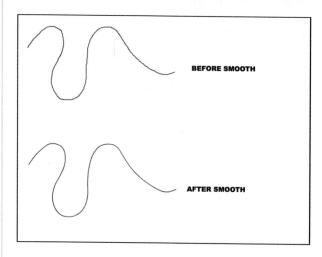

### ⑥ Use Ink Mode

Select **Ink** when you draw lines that are more complex. Flash smoothes your strokes only slightly, and your Pencil lines retain the shape you drew. Remember, though, that complex strokes contain many segments and are the most difficult to edit afterwards.

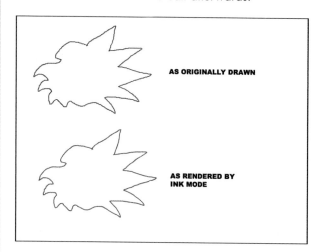

## 7 Draw the Line

After you select the pencil mode, simply click and drag the pencil on the Stage to draw your line. Depending on the mode you select, Flash straightens, smoothes, or renders the stroke when you release the mouse.

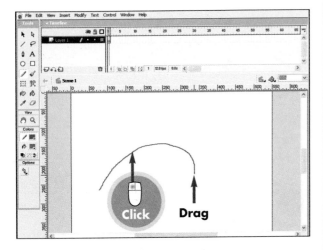

## 8 Select the Pen Tool

The Pen tool enables you to create lines and shapes with Bézier curves. Open shapes use the stroke color, and filled shapes use both the stroke and fill colors.

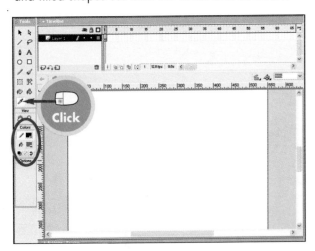

## 9 Create the First Segment

Click on the Stage with the Pen tool to place the first anchor point for a line segment. When you drag the mouse, you notice control point handles. Adjust the length and angle of the handles to determine the direction and length of the first curve.

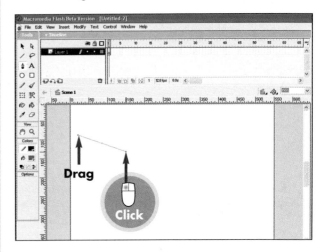

## 10 Add Additional Segments

Click again on the Stage to set another anchor point. A line appears to display the shape of the first curve. Click and drag the control handles for the second node to shape the first curve, and release the mouse to finalize the shape.

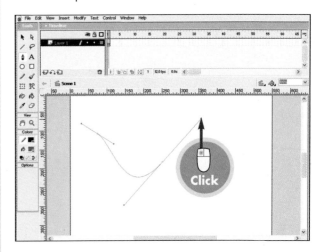

## ⑪ Complete an Open Path

To complete an open shape, double-click at the location where you want the path to end, or click the **Pen** tool in the toolbox.

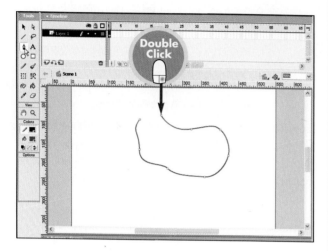

## ⑫ Complete a Closed Path

To complete a closed path, position the Pen tool over the first anchor point. When the cursor turns into a small loop, click or drag the Pen tool to close the path. The shape fills with the fill color when the path is closed. If desired, select the stroke and fill, and then select **Modify**, **Group** to group them.

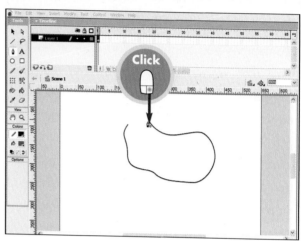

## Drawing Straight Lines with the Pen

Although the Line tool is designed to draw straight lines, you can also draw them with the Pen tool. Simply select the **Pen** tool, and click on the Stage to set the start and end points of the line.

# How to Edit and Reshape Lines

Sometimes you might need to edit or reshape lines after you create them. You can edit lines with either the Arrow tool or the Subselect tool, regardless of which tool you used to create the line. You can also use the Pen tool to add or delete nodes from an existing shape. Each tool uses a slightly different approach. One thing to remember when editing lines is that curved lines are usually composed of several segments, with very curvy lines containing more segments than lines that curve only slightly. In addition, you'll probably see more segments in lines created with the Pencil tool than those created with the Pen tool. It can help somewhat to optimize shapes (see Task 11, "How to Smooth and Optimize Shapes") before you edit them.

## 1 Select the Arrow Tool

Select the **Arrow** tool from the toolbox. Move the cursor toward any line, whether it was created with the Pencil tool or the Pen tool. You will see a small curve appear beside the cursor.

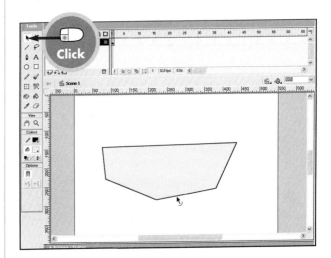

## ② Drag the Curve

While the curve appears beside the cursor, click and drag the curve to reshape it. If the curve is part of a filled shape, the fill will adjust to the shape of the new line after you release the mouse.

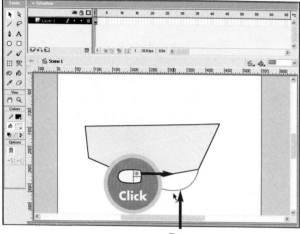

**Drag**

## ③ Split a Line Segment

If you find that the segment is too large to achieve the shape you want to achieve, you can use the Pencil or Line tool to split the segment. Simply draw a small line across the shape at the location where you want it to split.

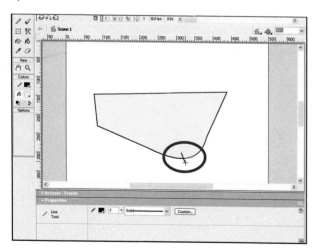

## ④ Erase the Split

After you reshape your object, you must delete two segments of the small line you drew to make the split (one segment will be outside the shape and the other inside the shape). Click to select a segment, and then delete it.

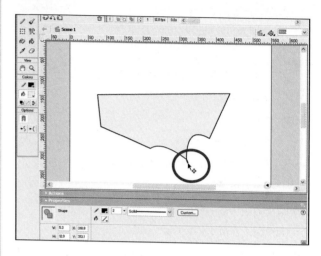

## ⑤ Select an Object with the Subselect Tool

The Subselect tool appears immediately to the right of the Arrow tool in the toolbox. When you use it to select the line you want to edit, the control nodes for the line or shape appear.

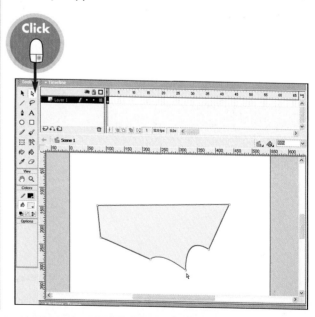

## 6 Select Anchor Points

Click an anchor point to select it; then **Shift-click** to select additional anchor points. Alternatively, you can draw a rectangular marquee with the Subselect tool to select several anchor points at the same time.

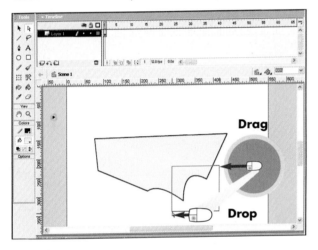

## 7 Reshape the Line

After you select an anchor point, its control nodes appear. Use the control nodes to reshape the line to your liking. After you reshape your object, click on the Stage to deselect it.

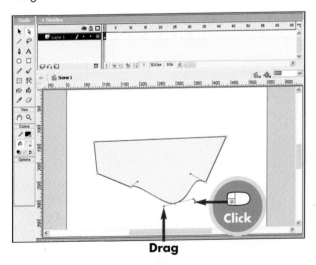

## 8 Convert a Corner Point to a Curve

Curves can include two types of anchor points. *Corner* points (indicated with a square node) appear when two line segments intersect at an angle. Corner points do not have tangent handles. To convert a corner point to a curve point, (**Option-drag**) [**Alt+drag**] with the Subselect tool.

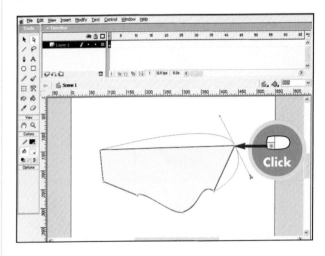

## 9 Convert a Curve Point to a Corner Point

A *curve* point (indicated with a circular node) appears when the two intersecting lines make a smooth curve. To convert a curve point to a corner point, hold down the (**Option**) [**Alt**] key and click the point once with the Subselect tool. The shape adjusts accordingly.

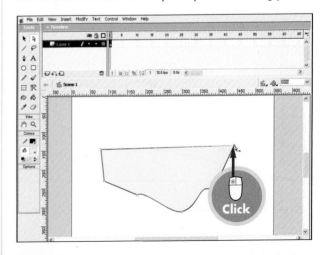

## ⑩ Add an Anchor Point

Use the Pen tool to add or delete nodes from the shape. Select the **Pen** tool from the Tools panel, and click to select the line or shape you want to edit. To add a new anchor point, place the cursor over the line at the desired location. When a small plus sign appears beside the cursor, click to add the point.

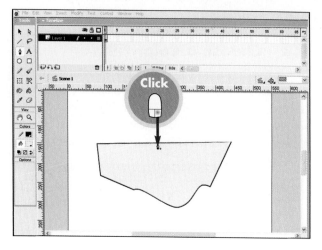

## ⑪ Delete an Anchor Point

To delete an anchor point, click the line to display the nodes if they do not already appear. Then position the Pen tool over an existing node. You might need to click more than once until the cursor displays a minus sign. The next click after you see the minus sign deletes the node.

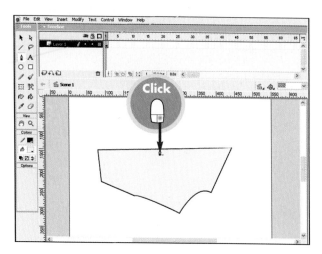

## ⑫ Nudge Anchor Points

You can use the arrow keys on your keyboard to nudge anchor points to a new location. With the Subselect tool, select the point(s) you want to move. Then use the Up, Down, Left, or Right arrow key to nudge the anchor point 1 pixel at a time.

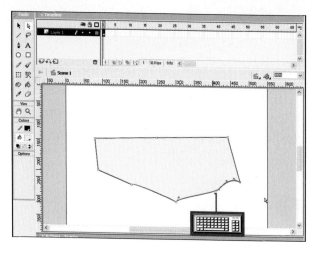

## How to Hint

### Changing the Pen Cursor

The Pen tool uses one of two types of cursors. You can use the Caps Lock key to toggle between the standard Pen tool cursor and a crosshair cursor. The crosshair cursor can help you place your lines more accurately. Press the **Caps Lock** key once to switch to the other cursor type, and press the **Caps Lock** key again to switch back to the original cursor. The cursor will change after you move the mouse.

# How to Draw and Reshape Fills

The Brush tool uses the fill color. You can use it to draw fills and set it so that it responds to a pressure-sensitive tablet. After you draw fills, you can reshape them using methods similar to reshaping lines.

## ① Select the Brush

Select the **Brush** tool from the toolbox. The Brush tool options appear in the Options section of the toolbox.

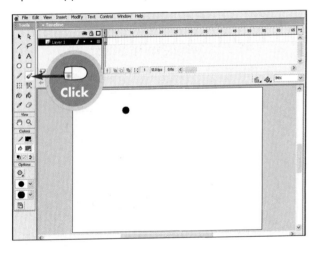

## ② Choose a Color Fill

To paint with a solid color, click the fill color square to select a color from your current palette. Alternatively, select a color or enter **Red**, **Green**, **Blue**, and **Alpha** values in the Color Mixer (select **Window**, **Color Mixer** or press **Shift+F9** if it is not displayed).

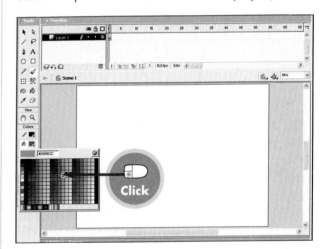

## ③ Select a Gradient Fill

To paint with a gradient fill, select **Linear** or **Radial** from the **Fill Style** drop-down list in the Color Mixer. Click a color indicator on the gradient bar, and select a color from either the color matrix or the color square at the right of the Fill Style drop-down list. Reposition the indicators as necessary to adjust the smoothness of the gradient.

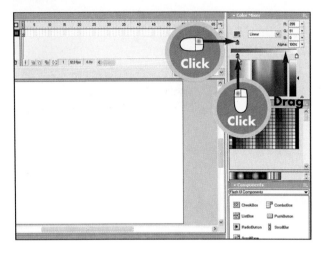

## ④ Select a Bitmap Fill

To paint with a bitmap fill, select **Bitmap** from the **Fill Style** drop-down list in the Color Mixer. If there are bitmap images in your library, small thumbnails appear in the Color Mixer. Click one of the thumbnails to select it. See Task 17, "How to Fill Shapes with Bitmaps"; Task 18, "How to Paint with a Bitmap"; and Task 19, "How to Set Bitmap Properties."

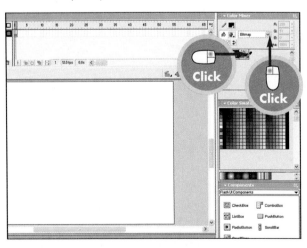

## ⑤ Select a Painting Mode

Click the **Brush Mode** modifier in the Options panel to select a painting mode: Paint Normal (covers everything), Paint Fills (leaves strokes untouched), Paint Behind (paints behind existing strokes and fills), Paint Selection (paints inside a selected fill), and Paint Inside (stays inside the lines).

## ⑥ Select the Brush Size

Click the **Brush Size** modifier in the Options panel to select one of 10 existing brush sizes.

## **9** Paint on the Stage

After you select your Brush tool options, paint on the Stage to draw your fill shape.

## **7** the Brush Shape

Select a brush shape from the **Brush Shape** modifier in the Options panel. Brush shapes include circular, elliptical, square, rectangular, and angled lines. Sample strokes are shown from left to right and then from top to bottom for the order in which the brush shapes appear in the drop-down list.

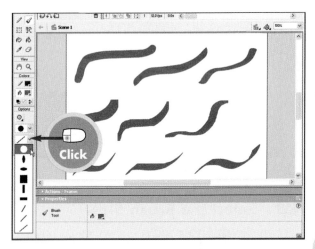

## **10** Reshape Fills

You can reshape fills in the same way you reshape lines. Select the **Arrow** tool, and then move the cursor toward the fill until you see a curve beside the cursor.

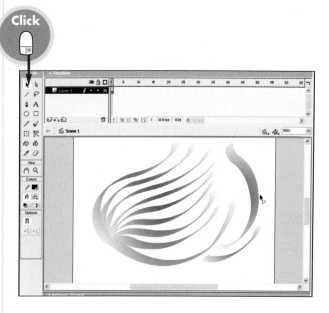

## **8** Enable the Lock Fill Modifier

If you are painting with a gradient fill, the Lock Fill modifier enables you to span the fill across several objects rather than sizing the gradient to fill one object.

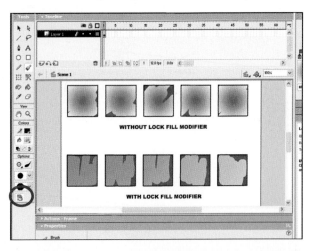

## ⑪ Drag the Outline

Click and drag the outline to reshape the fill.

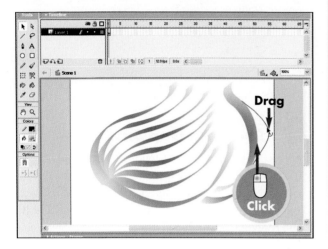

## ⑫ Release the Mouse Button

When you release the mouse button, the fill assumes the new shape.

## ⑬ Reshape with the Subselect Tool

You can also reshape your brush strokes with the Subselect tool. Follow the same procedures as discussed in Task 8, "How to Edit and Reshape Lines."

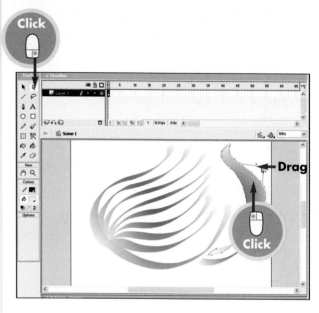

## Using a Pressure-Sensitive Tablet

If you are using a pressure-sensitive tablet, an additional option appears in the Options panel. Click the **Pressure** icon to take advantage of your tablet. Flash will vary the width of your stroke as you vary the pressure.

## Creating Multicolored Gradients

You can add more color indicators to the color bar in the Color Mixer to create gradients with more than two colors. Simply click in the color bar at the point at which you want to add another indicator. Then select a color for the indicator as usual. To delete a color indicator, drag it down off the color bar.

# How to Change Outlines and Fills

The Ink Bottle and Paint Bucket tools can be used to change the color and appearance of existing lines and fills. Use the Eyedropper tool to copy existing strokes or fills to another object. You can also use the Fill Transform tool to alter the appearance of gradient fills. The following steps show you how to perform these changes.

## 1 Use the Paint Bucket

You can use the Paint Bucket to fill shapes, including shapes that contain small gaps in the outlines. First, select the **Paint Bucket** from the Tools panel. Then, select a fill color, gradient, or bitmap fill as discussed in Task 9, "How to Draw and Reshape Fills."

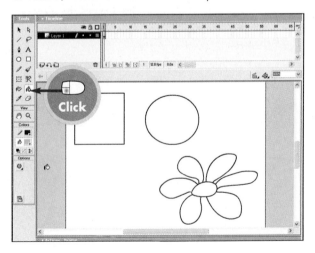

## 2 Choose a Gap Size

The Gap Size option in the Options palette enables you to control how much of a gap the Paint Bucket tool recognizes before it considers a shape to be closed. Choices are Don't Close Gaps, Close Small Gaps, Close Medium Gaps, and Close Large Gaps. Select the option that best applies to the shapes you want to fill.

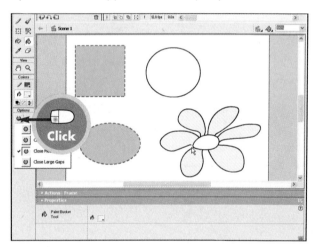

## ③ Click to Fill

To change the fill of an object that already has a fill, click the current fill to apply the new properties. To fill an enclosed area that is empty (as shown in this example), click inside the enclosed area.

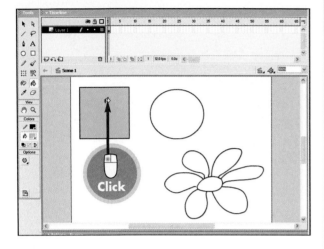

## ④ Lock the Fill

Similar to the Lock Fill modifier discussed for the Brush tool in Task 9, "How to Draw and Reshape Fills," the Paint Bucket also has a Lock Fill modifier. Use this modifier to span a gradient fill across several shapes.

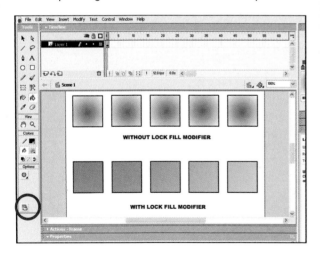

## ⑤ Use the Ink Bottle Tool

The Ink Bottle tool enables you to change existing outlines or to add outlines to a shape that does not already have an outline. First, select the **Ink Bottle** tool from the toolbox. Then, select your stroke properties, as discussed in Task 6, "How to Create and Group Shapes and Strokes."

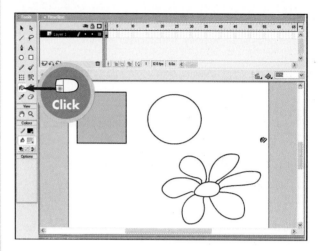

## ⑥ Change an Existing Stroke

You can use the Ink Bottle tool to change the width, color, or style of existing strokes. After you choose the new stroke size, color, or style, simply click the existing stroke with the Ink Bottle tool. The new properties will be applied to the existing stroke.

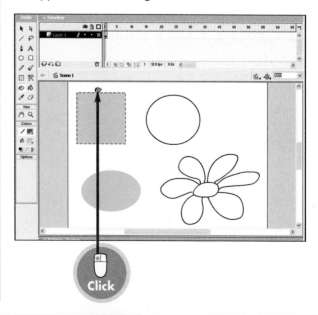

## ⑦ Add Strokes

To add a stroke to a shape that does not have one, click the outer edge of an existing fill with the Ink Bottle tool. Flash draws a stroke around the shape using the properties that are currently selected for the Ink Bottle tool.

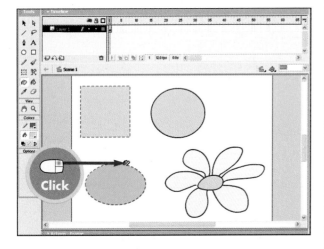

## ⑧ Copy a Fill

To copy a fill from one object to another, select the **Dropper** tool from the toolbox. Hover the cursor over the fill you want to copy. When you see a small brush icon, click the fill to copy its properties. The cursor then changes to a paint bucket.

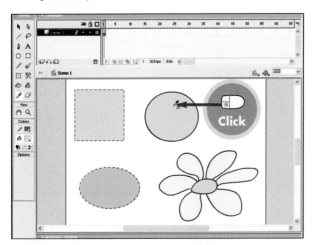

## ⑨ Apply the Copied Fill

Click the fill of the object(s) you want to change. After you apply the copied fill to the object you want to change, simply select another tool from the toolbox to exit the copy mode.

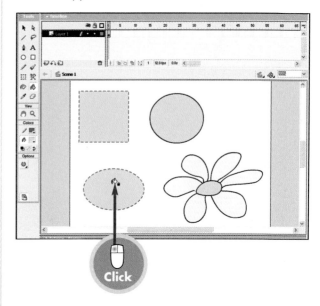

## ⑩ Copy a Stroke

To copy the properties of a stroke, select the **Dropper** tool from the toolbox. Hover the cursor over an existing stroke until you see a small Pencil icon. Then click the stroke to copy its properties.

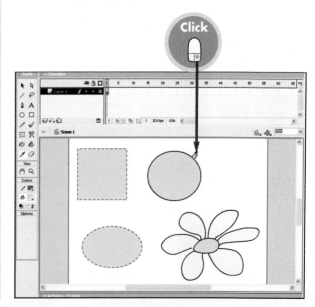

## ⓫ Apply the Copied Stroke

After you copy the stroke, the cursor turns into a paint bucket. Simply click the stroke for the object you want to change to apply the copied stroke properties.

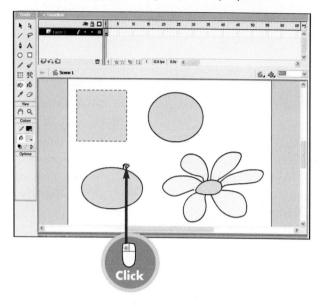

## ⓬ Adjust a Radial Gradient

To adjust a radial gradient fill, select the **Fill Transform** tool from the Tools panel. Click the gradient to reveal the transform controls; the center handle adjusts the center position. Three handles appear on the outer circle: the square handle adjusts width, the middle handle adjusts size, and the bottom handle adjusts rotation.

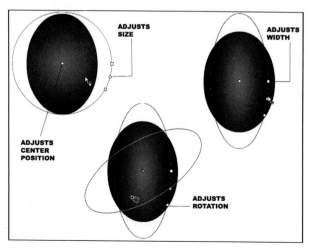

## ⓭ Adjust a Linear Gradient

To adjust a linear gradient, select the **Fill Transform** tool. The center handle adjusts the center point of the gradient. The circular handle in the corner adjusts the rotation of the gradient. The square handle on the side adjusts the width of the gradient.

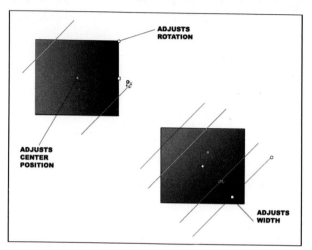

## Converting Lines to Fills

Flash also provides a command that enables you to convert lines to fills. Select the strokes you want to change, and then select **Modify**, **Shape**, **Convert Lines to Fills**.

## Enlarging or Reducing a Fill

You can increase or decrease the size of a fill by a fixed number of pixels. To do so, select **Modify**, **Shape**, **Expand Fill**. Next, enter the number of pixels in the **Distance** field. Then select either **Expand** to enlarge the fill or **Inset** to reduce the fill by the specified number of pixels.

# How to Smooth and Optimize Shapes

As you develop the symbols for your movies, you can keep the file sizes down if you keep your shapes smooth and made of the fewest number of curves possible. You've already learned that you can select different modes for the Pencil tool that help you smooth your shapes, and the Pen tool economizes on the number of curves by its very nature. But when you import shapes created in other programs, you might need to remove unnecessary curves. Flash provides commands that help optimize shapes even further, and they are discussed here.

## 1 Smooth Shapes and Lines

The Smooth command helps get rid of the jagged appearance of lines and shapes. To smooth shapes or lines, select one or more with the Arrow tool. Then, select **Modify**, **Smooth**. The more you smooth the shape, the more economical your movie will be.

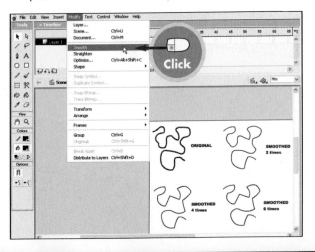

## 2 Straighten Shapes and Lines

The Straighten command is similar to the Smooth command. It smoothes out curved lines, but if a line is nearly straight, the Smooth command straightens it completely. To straighten shapes or lines, select one or more with the Arrow tool; then select **Modify**, **Straighten**.

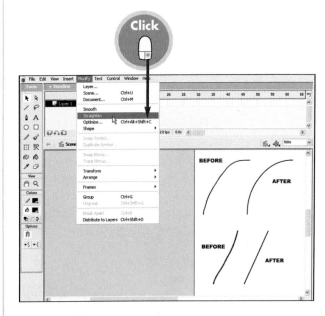

## How to Hint

### Optimization Versus Quality

Your results will vary depending on the curves with which you are working. Generally, the more you optimize your shapes, the less the results look like the original shapes. You will need to experiment to achieve the right balance between economy and quality.

## ③ Optimize Shapes

The Optimize command helps you achieve the perfect balance between appearance and economy. To optimize a shape or line, select the shape or shapes you want to optimize. Then select **Modify**, **Optimize**.

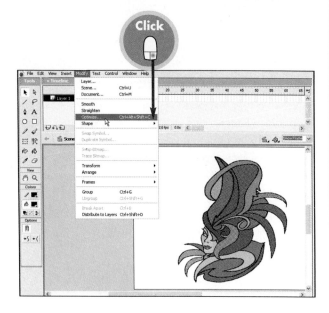

## ④ Set the Smoothing Amount

From the Optimize Curves dialog box, click and drag the **Smoothing** slider to set a smoothing amount between None and Maximum. The more you move the slider toward the Maximum setting, the smoother the curves will be. It also results in smaller file sizes.

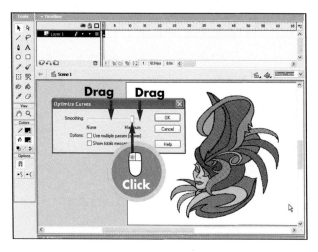

## ⑤ Additional Smoothing Options

Check the **Use Multiple Passes** option to automatically repeat the smoothing process until Flash fully optimizes the curves in your shape. Check the **Show Totals Message** option to display a size report after the smoothing process is complete.

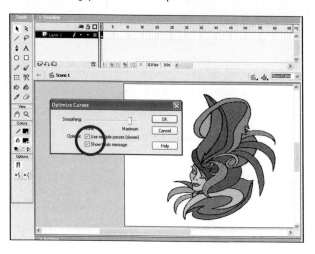

## ⑥ Complete the Optimization Process

Click **OK** to complete the optimization process. A summary of the optimization appears if you selected the option. Click **OK** to close the dialog box and view the results. If they are not what you expected, select **Edit**, **Undo** and repeat the process with a different setting.

# How to Set Type Attributes

**W**hen you select the Text tool, Flash provides several options in the Properties window that enable you to select a font and specify the size, color, and alignment properties. Other options enable you to increase the amount of space between characters, either automatically or manually (most commonly known as *kerning*). You can also adjust the amount of spacing used for right and left margins as well as other settings.

### ❶ Select the Text Tool

To add type, select the **Text** tool from the toolbox. The Properties window (⌘-**F3**) [**Ctrl+F3**] displays several options for your text. The settings in the top line control the font size, color, style, and alignment.

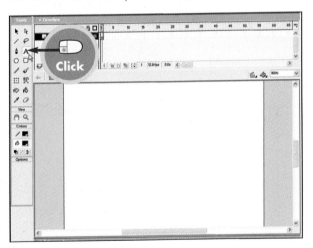

### ❷ Select Your Font

To select a font, expand the **Font** drop-down list in the Properties window, and drag your mouse over the font list until you find the font you want to use. A preview of the selected font appears in a flyout box. Click to select the font you want to use.

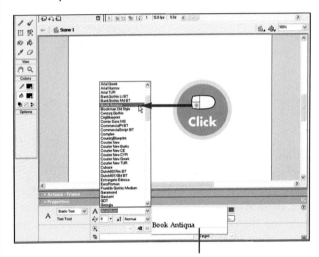

**Font Preview**

## ③ Select the Font Size

Use the Font Size box in the Properties window to enter a new point size. Alternatively, click the arrow to display the Font Size slider. Then click and drag the slider up or down to increase or decrease the font size.

## ④ Select the Text Color

To select a color for your text, click the **Text (Fill) Color** swatch to select a color from your current Flash palette. You can also select a new text color from the **Fill** color swatch in the Colors panel of the toolbox.

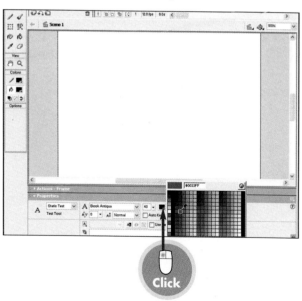

## ⑤ Select the Text Style

If available for the selected font, click the **Bold** button, **Italic** button, or both buttons to format the text further. Click the button again to turn off bold or italic.

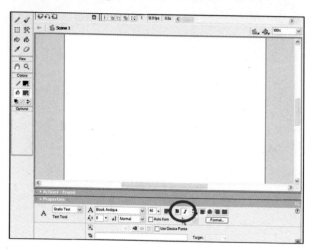

## ⑥ Align the Paragraphs

Click one of four alignment buttons to align your text: **Left/Top Justify**, **Center Justify**, **Right/Bottom Justify**, and **Full Justify**. You can now enter the text on your Stage unless you want to adjust character spacing, positioning, and kerning.

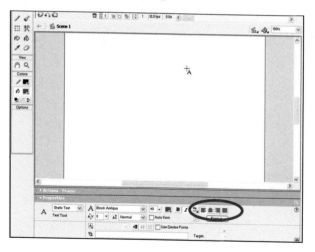

## 7 Change Letter Spacing

To increase or decrease the amount of spacing between letters, use the **Character Spacing** box. Click the arrow to use the **Tracking** slider. Move the slider up to increase the amount of space or down to decrease the amount of space between the letters. Alternatively, you can enter a number in the **Character Spacing** field.

## 8 Create Superscript or Subscript Text

Use the **Character Position** drop-down list to create superscript or subscript text. First, select the text you want to change. Then, select **Superscript** or **Subscript** from the drop-down menu. Select **Normal** to change the text back to its normal position.

## 9 Indent Paragraphs

To add an indentation to the first line in a paragraph, click the **Format** button to open the Format Options dialog box. To indent the first line of each paragraph, enter a pixel value greater than 0 (no indentation) in the **Indent** field.

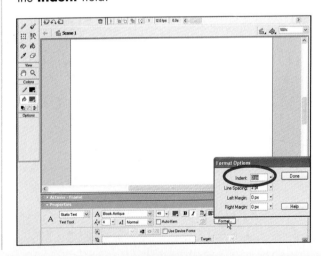

## ⑩ Adjust Line Spacing

The Format Options dialog box also includes a setting for Line Spacing. This setting controls the amount of space between the lines of text in your paragraphs. The default value for line spacing is 2 points. To increase the spacing, increase the setting. Negative numbers decrease the spacing between lines.

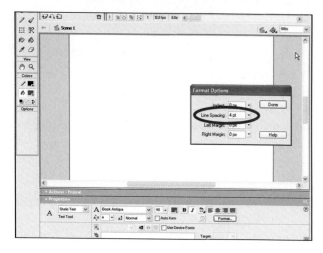

## ⑪ Adjust Margins

The Left and Right margin settings in the Format Options dialog box set the number of pixels from the text to the left and right edges of the text box. Increase the values to widen the left and right margins.

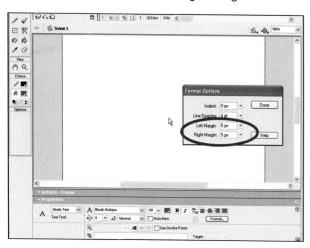

## ⑫ Enable or Disable Auto Kerning

Kerning controls the amount of space between certain pairs of letters. You might want to disable kerning for smaller text because reading kerned letters can sometimes be hard when the font size is small. To disable kerning, uncheck the **Auto Kern** option in the Properties window.

How to Hint

## Making a Statement

Line spacing, letter spacing, and kerning can make a difference in the way your text appears. Adding wide spaces between bold, dark letters can sometimes add an air of distinction and lighten up the look of your Flash movies.

## How to Tell Whether a Font Is Embedded

When you enter your text on the Stage, verify that it appears smoothed (or antialiased) after you type it. This indicates that Flash will embed the font so that other viewers will see the font properly when they play your movie. Your text appears rough or jagged when Flash can't embed the font in your movie. In that case, you can either select a different font or break the text apart into lines and fills.

# How to Add Text

Flash enables you to add three types of text fields: static, dynamic, and input. By default, Flash selects static text as the type of text you will enter. Static text content does not change, either dynamically or by user input. You can animate and apply effects to static text blocks just as you can with any other graphic element in your Flash movies. The other text choices, dynamic text and input text, are primarily for user interaction. They require scripting and techniques that go beyond the scope of this book and are not discussed here.

## Using Device Fonts

The Properties window also includes a Use Device Fonts option. Device fonts can decrease the file size of your movie and increase readability for small type sizes. When you enable this option, Flash does not embed the font for that text. Instead, Flash substitutes the closest device font that most resembles the font you select. Device fonts can also be selected from the font flyout menu (select **Text**, **Font**) and come in three types: sans, which most closely resembles fonts such as Arial or Helvetica; serif, which most closely resembles fonts such as Times New Roman; and typewriter, which resembles fixed-width fonts such as Courier or Courier New.

## ① Create Short Text Phrases

Select the **Text** tool from the toolbox and select your font properties (refer to Task 12, "How to Set Type Attributes"). Click the Stage where you want the text to appear and then type. The text field expands horizontally to fit the text on one line. To begin a new line, press (**Return**) [**Enter**]. Click outside the text box to finish.

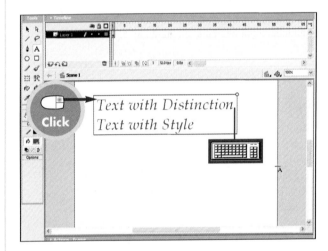

## ② Create Fixed-Width Paragraphs

To create a fixed-width text field, select the **Text** tool and select your font properties (refer to Task 12, "How to Set Type Attributes"). Click where you want the type to start. Drag to the desired width of the text block and release the mouse. The text wraps to fit the box as you type. Click outside the text box to finish.

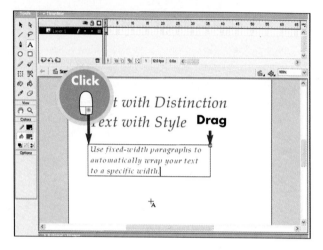

## ③ Change the Width of a Text Field

To change the width of a text field, click inside the text field with the Text tool to display the resize handle. Click and drag the resize handle and release at the desired width.

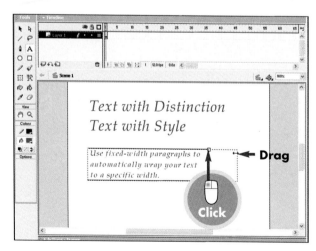

## ④ Reset to a Text Field

To remove the width setting from a fixed-width text field, select the **Text** tool. Click inside the text field to display the resize handle, which appears as a small square when the text box is fixed width. Then double-click the resize handle with the Text tool. The text field expands to fit the contents of the text field on one line.

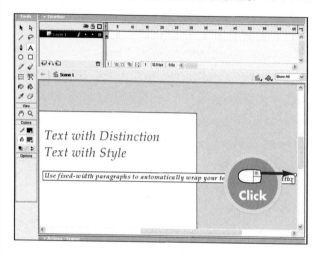

## ⑤ View All Text in Wide Text Fields

When a text block extends beyond the area you can see, select **View**, **Work Area**. Then, select **Show All** from the **Zoom** drop-down list in the upper-right corner of the Stage. After you zoom out, you can add line breaks or move the resize handle to resize the text field.

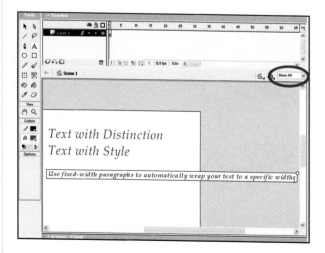

# How to Select and Edit Text

You can edit any text field in Flash as long as it has not been converted to shapes. To edit text, select a text block or specific text with the Text tool. After you select text for editing, you can change the font properties or edit the contents of the text field.

## ① Select All Text in a Text Field

To select all text in a text field, select the **Text** tool and click inside the text field to place the cursor. Then use the keyboard shortcut (⌘-**A**) [**Ctrl+A**] to select all text in the text field.

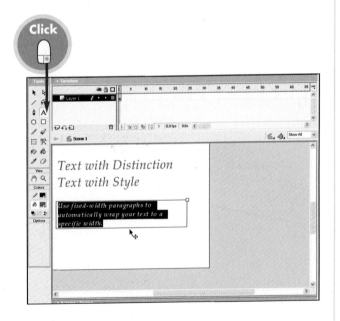

## ② Select Part of a Text Field

To select specific characters or words within a text field, select the **Text** tool and click inside the text field to place the cursor. Select text by dragging to select characters, double-clicking to select a word, or clicking at the beginning of the selection and Shift-clicking to end the selection.

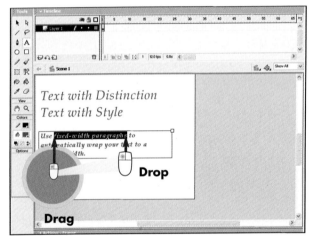

## 3 Select One or More Text Fields

To select one or more text fields for editing, select the **Arrow** tool from the toolbox. Then click a type block to select it. Shift-click to add additional text blocks to the selection.

## 4 Edit Selected Text

After you select text for editing, you can change the font, font size, color, style, and alignment using the same techniques you learned in Task 1, "Welcome to Flash."

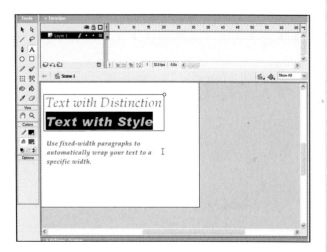

## 5 Use the Clipboard to Move Text

You can also use the Cut, Copy, and Paste commands to remove text or copy text elsewhere into your Flash projects. For example, you can cut some text from one text block and place it into another as shown here. You can also use the Clipboard to copy text from Flash into other applications or from other applications into Flash.

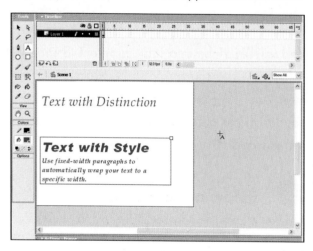

### How to Hint

## Creating Text with Drop Shadows

Flash does not create text with drop shadows automatically. An easy way to create drop-shadowed text is to select a text block with the Arrow tool. Select **Edit**, **Duplicate** to create a copy of the text. Reposition the duplicated text with the arrow keys if necessary, and change the color to the desired shadow color. Then select **Modify**, **Arrange**, **Send Backward** to move the shadow behind the foreground text. Finally, group the foreground text and shadow with the **Modify**, **Group** command.

# How to Convert and Reshape Text

If you want to reshape your text, you can convert any TrueType and PostScript font to shapes. Windows TrueType fonts can be broken apart to lines and fills you can reshape. For Mac users systems, PostScript fonts can be broken apart only if you are running Adobe Type Manager.

## 1 Select a Font

Use the Character panel to select a nice, bold font (such as Arial Black or something similar) in a large text size (48 points or higher). Enter text in a text field.

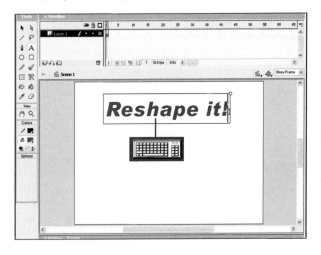

## 2 Break Text Apart

To convert the text to shapes that consist of lines and fills, select the text you want to change with the Arrow tool. Then select **Modify**, **Break Apart** or press (⌘-**B**) [**Ctrl+B**]. The first time you use this command each letter converts to a group; the second time converts the text to shapes.

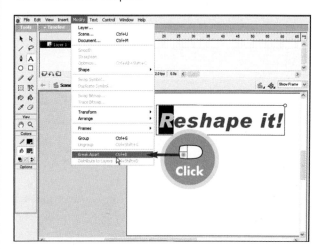

## How to Hint

### Ungrouping Grouped Text Symbols

To ungroup text symbols after you have grouped them, select **Modify**, **Ungroup**.

### Converting to a Symbol

After you break apart your text, it no longer responds to effects such as adjusting tint or alpha. To make it respond to these types of effects, you have to convert it into a symbol. After you group your text, select **Insert**, **Convert to Symbol** or press **F8** to convert the text to a Movie Clip, Button, or Graphic symbol.

## ③ Change Stroke Properties

After text is broken into shapes, you can choose a different color and width for the stroke. Select the **Ink Bottle** tool from the toolbox and use the **Properties** window to select a new color and width for the stroke as desired. In this example, a red stroke, one pixel in width, is selected. Click each letter to change its stroke to the new color and width.

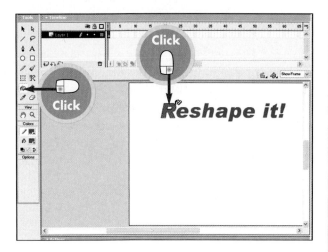

## ④ Change the Fill

Use the Arrow tool to marquee around all the letters in your text if they are not still selected. Then select **Radial Gradient** from the **Color Mixer**. Click each color marker to change the gradient colors (such as yellow and orange, as shown in this example). The text becomes filled with the gradient you design in the Fill panel.

## ⑤ Reshape Text Shapes

To reshape text, select the **Arrow** tool. Click away from the selected text to deselect it. Then drag the outline of the text to reshape the curves. As you drag the outline, the fill adjusts to fill the new shape of the text.

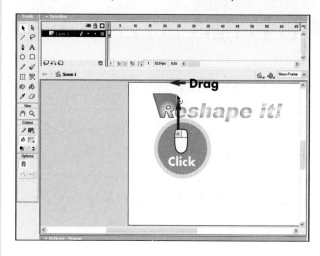

## ⑥ Group Text Shapes

After you break text apart, it exists as several individual shapes in your Flash movie. It is generally a good idea to group the individual letters back into the word or phrase you originally broke apart because doing so makes moving as a group easier. Select all the letters and select **Modify**, **Group** to combine the letters into a group.

# How to Import Bitmap Files into Macromedia Flash

**F**lash enables you to import a wide variety of bitmap file types (BMP, GIF, JPEG, and PNG images). Additional formats include MacPaint (.pntg), Photoshop (.psd), PICT (.pct, .pic), QuickTime Image (.qtif), Silicon Graphics (.sgi), TGA (.tga), and TIFF (.tif). Some of these formats require that you install QuickTime on your computer.

**1** **Select the Import Command**

To begin the import process, select **File**, **Import**. Alternatively, press the keyboard shortcut (⌘**-R**) [**Ctrl+R**]. This brings up the Import dialog box.

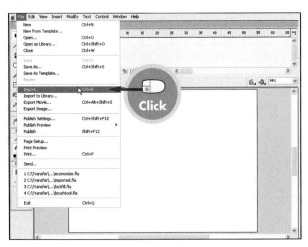

**2** **Select a File Format**

Click the **Files of Type** drop-down list (the **Show** drop-down list on Mac). This list displays all the file types you can import into Flash. If you know the file format of the file you want to import, select it from the list. This makes finding the file(s) you want much easier.

## ③ Select the File (PC)

On the PC, click the **Look In** drop-down list and navigate through the folders on your computer until you locate the file(s) you want to import. To import a range of files, click the name of the first file, hold down the **Shift** key, and click the last file. To import nonadjacent files, hold down **Ctrl** while clicking each individual filename.

## ④ Select the File (Mac)

On the Mac, navigate to the correct folder, click the name of each file you want to import, and click the **Add** button to add it to the list on the right. Remove files from the list by clicking **Remove**.

---

### How to Hint

### The Import to Library Command

You can also use the **File**, **Import to Library** command to import images. The steps are basically the same as outlined in this task, except that Flash does not place the images onto the Stage when it imports the images into the library.

### Watch Those File Sizes!

Using a lot of bitmaps increases the size of your Flash project and Flash movie, which can slow download. If you use bitmaps in your Flash movies, try to reduce file sizes before you import them. (Scaling the image down in your Flash movie will not reduce the byte size of the bitmap.)

---

## ⑤ Open the Selected File

On the PC, after you select the desired file, click the **Open** button to import the file. On the Mac, click the **Import** button. The file appears in the center of the Flash Stage.

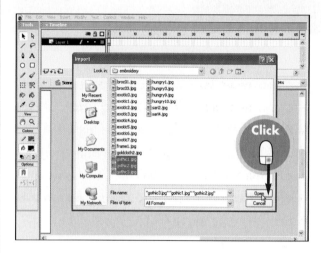

## ⑥ Use Copy and Paste

You can also use the Copy and Paste commands to import graphics. Open or create a bitmap in your favorite paint program, and then use the **Edit**, **Copy** command to copy it into the Clipboard. Next, switch to Flash. Click the Timeline at the frame and layer in which you want to place the bitmap, and select **Edit**, **Paste** to place the artwork on the Stage.

# How to Fill Shapes with Bitmaps

**W**hen you break apart an imported bitmap, you can fill ovals, rectangles, and brush strokes with a bitmap fill. You can also use the Lasso and Magic Wand tools to select and modify portions of a bitmap image. The following task shows you how to break apart a bitmap so you can use it as a fill.

## ❶ Open the Library

Open the Library to access the images you imported (see Task 16, "How to Import Bitmap Files into Flash"). When you click the image names, a preview appears in the Library window.

## ❷ Place an Image on the Stage

Drag and drop an image from the Library onto the Stage.

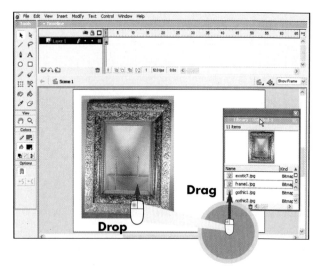

## ❸ Break Apart the Bitmap

With the bitmap selected, select **Modify**, **Break Apart** or use (⌘-**B**) [**Ctrl+B**] to break apart the bitmap.

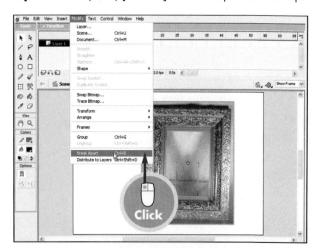

## ④ Use the Bitmap for a Fill

After you break apart a bitmap, small white dots fill the image as a visual indicator that the bitmap is broken apart. Now, select the **Dropper** tool and click the image with it. The cursor changes to a paint bucket, and a small thumbnail of the bitmap appears in the Fill color square in the Colors panel.

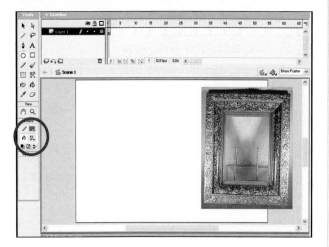

## ⑤ Draw a Shape

Select the **Oval** tool or **Rectangle** tool to draw an object on the Stage. Notice that the bitmap fills the object.

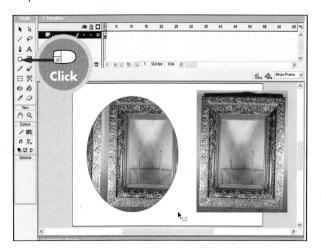

## ⑥ Delete the Broken-Apart Image

Delete the broken-apart image from the Stage. The filled object remains on the Stage.

# How to Paint with a Bitmap

As you learned in the previous task, you can fill rectangles, ovals, and other shapes with any bitmap you have imported into your Flash movie. One of the nicest features of Flash enables you to paint with a bitmap. This adds artistic flair to bitmap images. The following task demonstrates another way you can select a bitmap as a fill and shows you how to paint with a bitmap.

## ❶ Open the Library

If the library window is not open, select **Window**, **Library** to open it.

## ❷ Select the Bitmap

Click a bitmap name to view a preview of the image in the library. When you find the bitmap you want to use, drag and drop a copy of the bitmap onto the work area and rescale it if necessary.

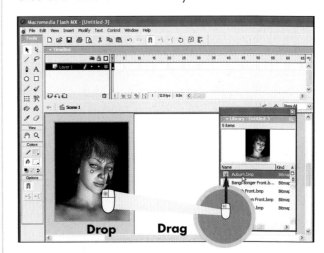

## ③ Break Apart the Bitmap

Click the bitmap with the **Arrow** tool to select it. Then select **Modify**, **Break Apart**. When the bitmap is broken apart, a dotted overlay appears above the bitmap.

## ④ Select the Fill with the Dropper

Select the **Dropper** tool from the **Tools** panel, and click the bitmap you broke apart. After you click the bitmap, it appears in the Colors panel as the selected fill. The cursor turns into a paint bucket, which you can use to fill areas with the bitmap. To paint with the bitmap, continue to the next step.

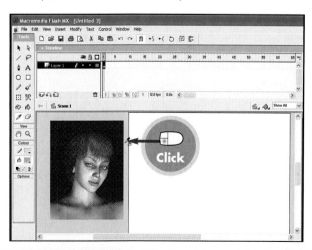

## ⑤ Select the Brush Tool and Paint

With the bitmap selected as the current fill, immediately select the **Brush** tool. Select your brush size from the **Options** palette. Then paint on the Stage with the brush. Initially, the bitmap does not appear in the stroke. Release the mouse to render the bitmap fill on the stroke.

How to Hint

## More About Bitmap Fills

When you paint or fill with a bitmap, the image tiles horizontally and vertically to fill the area. Use the eraser to remove unwanted areas of the strokes or fills.

## Using Solid Colors and Bitmap Fills Together

You can combine bitmap fills with solid color fills to create some interesting effects and patterns in your Flash movies. Use the **Brush** tool to paint with the bitmap to place an interesting shape on the Stage. Then select a solid color or gradient to paint over other areas in the bitmap. If you create the solid-colored strokes before you group the bitmap fill, you can also use solid-colored strokes or the Eraser tool to "cut out" areas of the bitmap fill.

# How to Set Bitmap Properties

The Bitmap Properties dialog box provides detailed information about the bitmap and enables you to make choices regarding file compression and antialiasing. This task explores the Bitmap Properties dialog box in detail.

**① Import a Bitmap to the Library**

Follow the steps outlined in Task 16, "How to Import Bitmap Files into Flash," to import one or more bitmaps into your library. If the library is not open, select **Window**, **Library** to open the library.

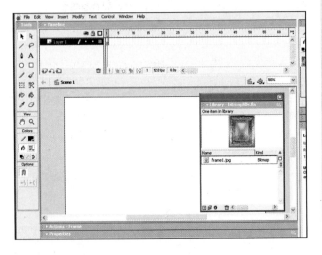

**② Open the Bitmap Properties**

Click the name of the bitmap whose properties you want to set. Then, click the **Properties** button (the icon with the small *i*) to open the Bitmap Properties dialog box. Alternatively, (double-click) [right-click] the image's name in the library list and select **Properties** from the menu, or select **Properties** from the **Options** drop-down list at the top of the Library window.

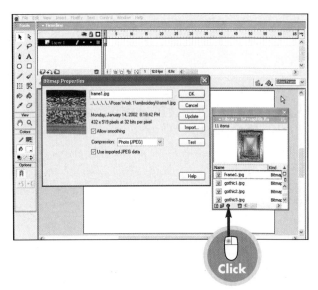

Click

## How to Hint

### Editing Bitmaps in an Image-Editing Program

If you want to use your favorite image-editing program to edit your bitmap, you can launch the editor directly from Flash. Right-click the bitmap icon in the Library window, and select **Edit With** (or **Edit with Fireworks** if you have Fireworks installed).

## ③ Set Antialiasing

Check the **Allow Smoothing** box to engage antialiasing. This helps the image appear smoother by softening the hard edges. Keep in mind that antialiased images have a larger file size than images that are not antialiased because of all the transitional colors created.

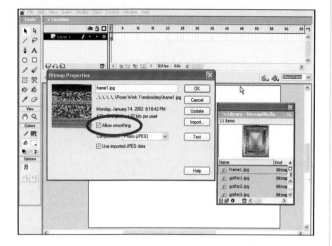

## ④ Select a Compression Setting

Click the **Compression** drop-down list to choose between Photo (JPEG) or Lossless (PNG/GIF). Select **Lossless (PNG/GIF)** for simple images that contain large blocks of solid colors; select **Photo (JPEG)** for images with many colors and color transition areas, such as full-color photographs. You also can click the **Use Imported JPEG Data** box to use the default quality.

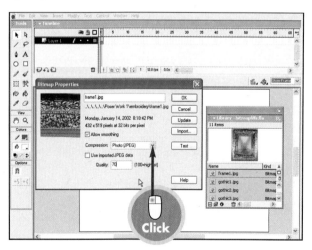

## ⑤ Test the File Compression Setting

Click the **Test** button to update the summary file information and the preview window when you change your JPEG compression settings. Summary information appears for JPEG images.

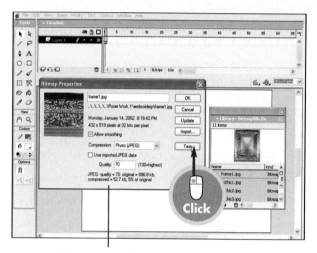

**Summary information**

## ⑥ Update a Bitmap Image

You can edit bitmaps in an external program after you add them to your library. When you do this, save the revised image over the previous version, using the same file location and filename. To update the image, right-click an image name in the library and select **Update** from the menu that appears. From the Update Library Items dialog box, select the images you need to update.

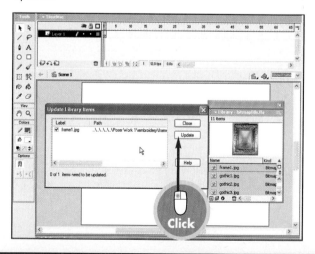

# How to Embed a Movie File

**E**ven though you were able to import movies into Flash in previous versions, this feature has been substantially improved in Flash MX. Now, Flash enables you to embed movie files directly into your Flash movies and use a new codec to stream the movies, along with other content, in your Flash movie. You can later publish the movie as a Flash movie (SWF) or a QuickTime movie (MOV).

## ① Import the Movie Clip

To import a video as an embedded clip, select **File**, **Import**. Select a movie file (**Video for Windows**, **Quick Time Movie, or MPEG Movie, Digital Video, Windows Media**, or **Macromedia Flash Video** format) and click **Open**.

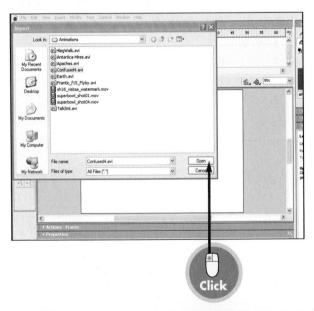

## ② Set Quality, Keyframe Interval, and Scale

From the Import Video Settings dialog box, enter or adjust the quality setting to control the amount of compression. Lower values produce smaller files. The Keyframe Interval value determines how often Flash stores a complete frame of video, and the Scale value reduces the dimensions of the video.

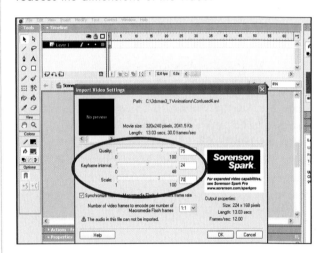

### How to Hint

## Editing the Clip with an External Editor

After you import a movie to your Flash project, you can edit it in an external editor. To update the movie in the Library, select the old version from the Library, and select **Properties** from the options menu in the Library panel. When the Embedded Video Properties dialog box appears, click **Update**.

## ③ Synchronize to Movie Speed

To match the video frame rate to your movie frame rate, select the **Synchronize Video to Macromedia Flash Document Frame Rate** option. Deselect this option to use the frame rate of the imported movie.

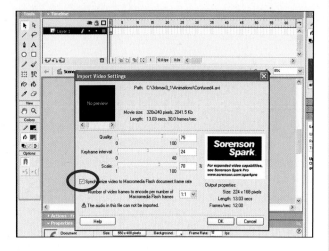

## ④ Set Encoding Ratio

To specify the ratio of imported video to Flash movie frame, enter or select a value for **Number of Video Frames to Encode per Number of Macromedia Flash Frames**. A 1:1 ratio encodes one imported video frame per Flash movie frame; a 1:2 ratio encodes one video frame for every two Flash movie frames.

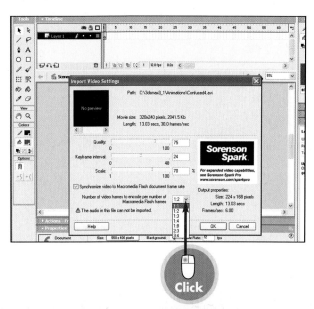

## ⑤ Import Audio

To include the audio track (if there is one), select the **Import Audio** option. Deselect this option to omit the audio. A warning appears in the Import Video Settings dialog box if you are unable to import the video from the file.

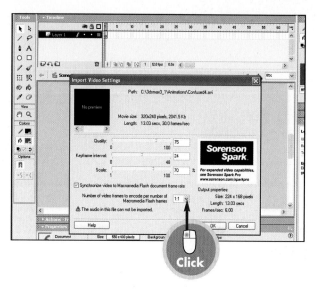

## ⑥ Finalize the Import

Click **OK** to import the video file. If you import the video directly to the Stage, a warning may advise you that the imported clip contains more frames than the existing movie. Click **Yes** to extend the movie frames to match the imported video, or click **No** to keep the Flash movie at its current size.

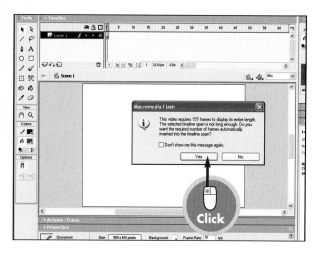

Task

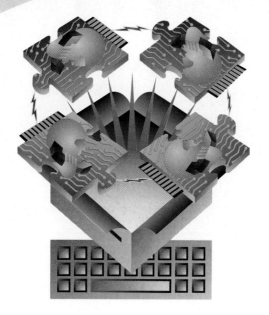

**2**

# Building and Editing Symbols

Every Flash project you create contains a library that can store the items used in your Flash movie. After you develop your objects, you can convert them to *symbols* and store them in the project library.

Flash uses three types of symbols. *Graphic symbols* are used for static images. *Movie Clips* are reusable pieces of animation that play independently of the main movie (somewhat like a movie within a movie). You can animate Movie Clips in a single frame and use action scripting to manipulate them in many ways. *Buttons*, the third type of Flash symbol, are discussed in more detail in Part 5, "Adding Navigation and Interactivity."

With wise planning and use of symbols, you can make movies that download and stream much more quickly. Use instances whenever you can. The key here is to economize on the elements that make up your movie.

# How to Convert Objects to Symbols

Before you perform some operations in Flash (such as tweening, which you'll learn more about in Part 3, "Basic Animation"), you might need to convert your objects to symbols. You can convert any object on your Stage into a symbol. In this task, you'll create a simple object on the Stage and then convert it to a symbol.

## ① Draw an Object on the Stage

Select the Brush tool from the toolbox, and select your desired fill color from the color palette. Draw a footprint on the Stage.

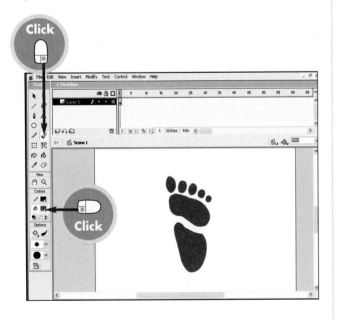

## ② Select the Objects

Use the Arrow tool or Lasso tool to draw a selection area around the objects.

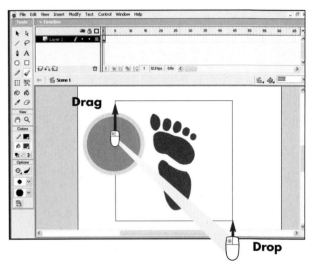

## ③ Convert the Objects to a Symbol

Select **Insert**, **Convert to Symbol**, or press **F8** on your keyboard. The **Symbol Properties** dialog box appears.

## ④ Name the Symbol and Choose Its Behavior

Enter a name for the symbol (such as **Footprint**) in the **Name** field. Next, select the **Behavior** radio button (**Movie Clip**, **Button**, or **Graphic**) that corresponds to the type of symbol you want to create. For this example, select **Graphic**.

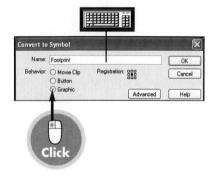

## ⑤ Complete the Symbol

Click **OK** to convert the object to a symbol. Flash places the master symbol in the Library (to see it, select **Window**, **Library** or press **F11** to open the library, then click the symbol name). The original item that you created is now an instance of the symbol that remains on the Stage.

# How to Create a New Symbol

**A**nother way to create a symbol is to begin with an empty symbol and build your symbols directly in symbol-editing mode. **Insert**, **New Symbol** allows you to build a symbol in this manner when you follow these steps.

## ① Select Insert, New Symbol

If you already have other objects on the Stage, make sure that none of them are selected. Then, select **Insert, New Symbol**, or use the keyboard shortcut (⌘-**F8**) on a Mac, [**Ctrl+F8**] in Windows.

## ② Name the Symbol

In the **Symbol Properties** dialog box, enter a unique name for your symbol (such as **Shoe**, shown here). If you enter a symbol name that already appears in your movie library, Flash prompts you to use a different name.

## ③ Choose a Behavior and Click OK

Select **Movie Clip**, **Button**, or **Graphic** for the behavior type (for this example, select **Graphic**); then click **OK** to exit the **Symbol Properties** dialog box.

## ④ Enter Symbol-Editing Mode

The Timeline should now display a new tab named Shoe, which tells you that you are in symbol-editing mode for your Shoe symbol. The Timeline displays one layer named Layer 1. A crosshair, which marks the registration (or center) point of the symbol, appears on the Stage. Now you can create the master symbol.

**Symbol tab**

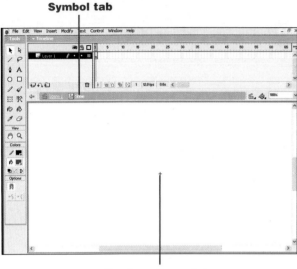

**Registration point**

## ⑤ Develop Your Symbol

Develop your symbol using drawing and text tools, imported objects, or other symbols from your library. Use multiple layers if desired. Note in the case of this example that graphic symbols should contain only one frame.

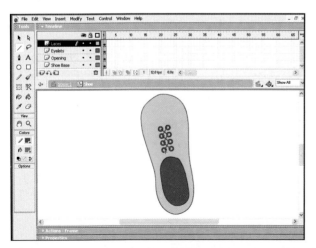

## ⑥ Exit Symbol-Editing Mode

To exit symbol-editing mode, click the **Scene** tab above the Timeline (located to the left of the Shoe tab); or you can select **Edit**, **Edit Document** or use the shortcut (⌘-E) on Mac, [**Ctrl+E**] in Windows.

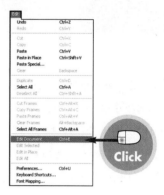

**How to Hint**

## Converting Multiple-Layered Objects to Symbols

When you create an object that has multiple layers, Flash merges them into a single layer when you convert the object to a symbol. The easiest way to create a multilayered symbol is to use the method outlined in Task 2 to create a new symbol and add additional layers while you are in symbol-editing mode.

# How to Use the Library

As the number of symbols in your movie increases, the Library includes features that are especially useful, because you can organize them into folders, assign useful names to them, and sort the symbols in various ways. It also keeps track of the number of times each symbol appears in your current project. Flash also enables you to use shared libraries that let you use symbols in multiple projects. When you edit any master symbol in a shared library, Flash updates the symbol in every project in which the symbol appears, saving a lot of time and effort.

## ① Open the Library

To open the Library for your current project, select **Window**, **Library**. Alternatively, use the keyboard shortcut **F11**. A check mark appears beside the command when the Library window is open.

## ② Resize the Library Window

You can resize the Library window to display additional columns. Position the cursor over any edge or corner of the window. When a double arrow cursor appears, click and drag in the direction indicated. You can also click the **Wide Library View** button to display all the columns in the library or click the **Narrow Library View** button to display only the Name column.

**Drag**

## How to Hint

### Renaming Library Items

To rename a Library item, double-click the item name or select the item you want to rename, and select **Rename** from the **Library Options** menu. Enter a new name, and press **Enter** or **Return** to assign it. You can also click the **Information** icon at the bottom of the Library window to rename the item in the **Symbol Properties** dialog box.

## ③ Resize the Column Widths

To resize Library column widths while in Wide Library View as described in the previous step, position the cursor between column headers; then, click and drag left or right to resize the columns.

## ⑤ Move Objects Between Folders

To move objects into folders, or from one folder to another, highlight one or more objects. Then, drag them to the new folder and release the mouse button.

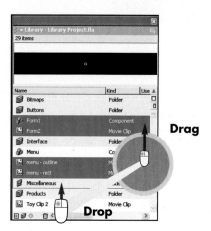

## ④ Create Folders

Folders help you organize the symbols into logical groups. To create a folder, click the **New Folder** button at the bottom of the Library window or select **New Folder** from the **Library Options** menu. Enter a name for the new folder, and press **Enter** or **Return** to assign the name (**Miscellaneous** in this case).

## ⑥ Sort Objects in Folders

Buttons at the top of the right scrollbar enable you to view the library in Wide or Narrow view. With the Library in Wide state, click the appropriate column header to sort contents by Name, Kind, Use Count, Linkage, or Date Modified. Click the **Triangle** button at the right edge of the column headers to toggle the sorting between ascending and descending alphabetical order.

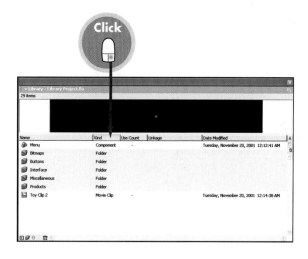

# How to Add Symbols to Your Movie

**A**fter you add symbols to your library, adding them to your movie is a relatively easy process. Simply select a symbol from your movie library and drag it onto the Stage. You can also copy and paste symbols to create additional instances or to move symbols between layers. Flash also lets you use symbols from other movie libraries.

**1** **Insert a Symbol from the Library**

Select **Window, Library,** or use the shortcut (⌘-**L**) on Mac, [**Ctrl+L**] in Windows to open your movie library. As you click the symbols in the Library, a preview appears in the preview window. Drag either the name of the selected symbol or its preview image to the Stage, and release the mouse button.

**2** **Copy and Paste Symbols**

You can also use the Copy and Paste commands to create a new instance of a symbol on the Stage. Select the symbol you want to copy, and select **Edit**, **Copy** to copy it onto the Clipboard. Then, select **Edit**, **Paste** to paste the symbol into the center of the Stage. Windows users can also use the **Copy** and **Paste** buttons on the standard toolbar.

## ③ Move Symbols to Another Layer

You can also use the Clipboard to move an object from one layer to another. Select the symbol you want to move. Then, select **Edit**, **Cut** to remove it from the stage and place it onto the Clipboard. Switch to another layer, and select **Edit**, **Paste in Place**. The symbol appears in the new layer at the same coordinates.

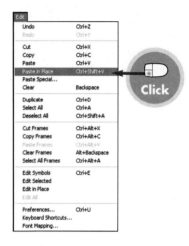

## ④ Use Symbols from Other Movies

To use symbols from other Flash movies you have already created, select **File, Open As Library** to display the **Open As Library** dialog box.

## ⑤ Locate the Movie File

Locate the movie that contains the symbols you want to place into your current movie. Next, select **Open** to display the library for that project. Click and drag symbols from this library onto your Stage. Flash displays all open libraries in a single Library window, and you can drag and drop symbols between them if desired.

How to Hint

## Using Multiple Libraries

Flash MX displays the libraries for all open movies in a single Library panel. A gray bar, which displays the name of the associated movie, appears at the top of each open library section. You can drag and drop symbols from any open library into your current project, or drag and drop symbols and folders between libraries. To collapse or expand the library, click the arrow at the left of the library name in the gray bar. To close a library, right-click the gray bar and choose Close Panel from the menu that appears.

## Creating a Master Symbol Library

Even though you can use symbols from any movie library, it makes sense to create special libraries for symbols you use repeatedly. For example, create a folder named Master Libraries in your Flash installation folder and store all your symbol libraries there, using movie names such as `Buttons.fla`, `Movie Clips.fla`, and so on.

# How to Edit Symbols

**Occasionally**, you need to change the color or artwork of a symbol after you create it. There are a number of ways that you can change a symbol that is already on the Stage. The following task demonstrates the many ways in which you can edit a symbol.

**1 Edit a Symbol from the Library**

To edit a symbol from the movie library, right-click (**Ctrl-click** for the Mac) the name of the symbol you want to change and select **Edit** from the menu that appears. The symbol opens in symbol-editing mode.

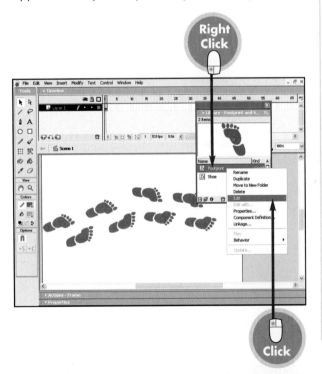

**2 Return to the Stage**

After you make changes to the symbol, select **Edit**, **Edit Document** or use the keyboard shortcut (⌘-**E**) on Mac, [**Ctrl+E**] in Windows to return to your movie's Stage. Any instances on the Stage that are linked to the symbol will reflect the changes you made.

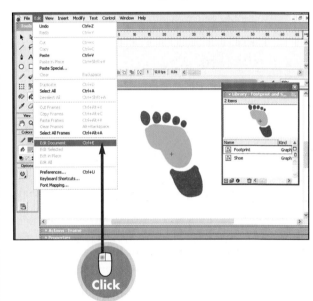

## ③ Edit a Symbol from the Stage

Alternatively, you can enter symbol-editing mode from the Stage. Right-click (Ctrl-click for Mac) the symbol you want to change, and select **Edit** from the menu that appears. The symbol opens in symbol-editing mode. Select **Edit**, **Edit Movie** or use the shortcut (⌘-**E**) [**Ctrl+E**] to return to your movie's Stage after you finish editing.

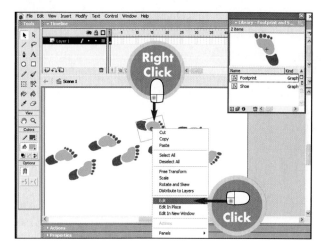

## ④ Edit a Symbol in Place

Sometimes, you need to make changes to a symbol while you also see the other objects that surround it. The easiest way to do this is to double-click a symbol on the Stage. You can also right-click (Ctrl-click for Mac) any symbol on the Stage and select **Edit in Place** from the menu. The surrounding artwork dims behind the symbol you are editing.

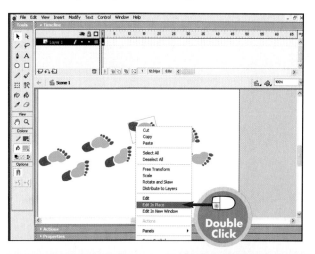

## ⑤ Edit in a New Window

To edit a symbol in a window that is totally separate from the Stage, right-click (Ctrl-click) a symbol on the Stage and select **Edit in New Window**. The new window displays only the symbol that you selected while the movie remains open in its original window. Click the **Close** button in the upper-right corner of the symbol window when your edits are complete.

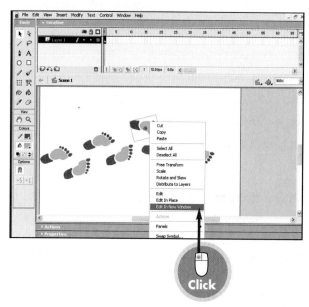

## How to Hint

### Editing Symbols Saves Time!

If you already have a symbol in another movie that is close in appearance to a new symbol you want to create, by all means, use it! After you add the symbol to your current project, you can treat it the same way as any other symbol in your movie.

# How to Convert Symbol Behaviors

Occasionally, you might need to convert between symbol behaviors. For example, you might initially create a Graphic symbol and find later that you want to convert it to a Movie Clip or Button. This task shows you how to convert between symbol behaviors.

## 1 Open the Movie's Library

Open the project that contains the symbol you want to change. If your movie library is not open, select **Window**, **Library** or use the keyboard shortcut **F11** to open it.

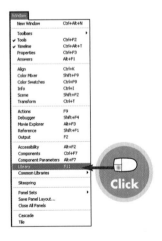

## 2 Select the Symbol from the Library

Click the symbol name in the Library to highlight the symbol you want to change. A picture of the symbol appears in the preview pane.

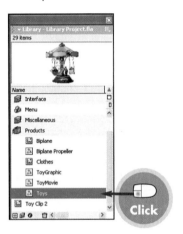

## ③ Select a New Behavior (Method 1)

In the Library, right-click (Ctrl-click on the Mac) the symbol name to open the Library options menu. Select **Behavior** from the menu that appears, and drag the mouse to select a new symbol behavior. Any instances already on the Stage will retain their original behaviors, but all new instances dragged from the Library will use the new behavior.

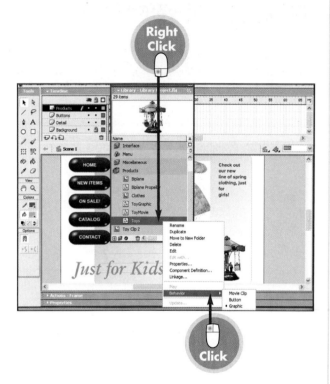

## ④ Select a New Behavior (Method 2)

To select a new behavior and optionally rename the symbol, right-click (Ctrl-click on the Mac) a symbol in the Library. Select **Properties** from the menu that appears to display the **Symbol Properties** dialog box. If desired, enter a new name for the symbol and select the new behavior type. Then, click **OK** to apply the changes. Any instances already on the Stage will retain their original behaviors. All new instances dragged from the Library, however, will change to reflect this new behavior.

### Duplicating a Symbol

How to Hint

If you want to keep the original symbol as it is, you can create a duplicate of the symbol and change the default behavior of the duplicate. To duplicate a symbol, right-click the original symbol in the Library and select **Duplicate** from the menu that appears. Flash initially names the symbol *Symbol Name* copy, where *Symbol Name* is the name of the original symbol. Rename the symbol as you choose, and then select a new default behavior for the copy.

# How to Change Instance Colors

The Effect panel offers several options that change the appearance of an instance. You can adjust the brightness, tint, or transparency of an instance without affecting the other instances on the Stage.

## 1 Open the Properties Window

With the Arrow tool, click an instance on the Stage to select it. If necessary, select **Window**, **Properties** or press (⌘-**F3**) [**Ctrl+F3**] to open the Properties window.

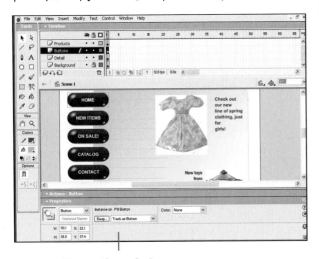

Properties window

## 2 Change the Brightness of an Instance

To change the brightness of an instance, select **Brightness** from the **Color** drop-down list. Move the **Brightness** slider down to darken the color or up to brighten it. Alternatively, enter a numerical value between −**100** (black) and +**100** (white) in the **Brightness** field, and press (**Return**) [**Enter**]. A brightness setting of **0** returns the symbol to its original level.

## 3. Change the Tint of an Instance

To tint the instance with another color, select **Tint** from the **Color** drop-down list. Click the color selector at the right of the drop-down list, and use the crosshair cursor to select a new color; or enter numerical values in the **R**, **G**, and **B** fields. Use the slider at the right of the **Effect** drop-down list to adjust the amount of tint.

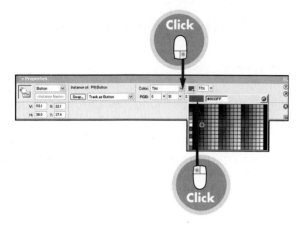

## 4. Change the Transparency of an Instance

To change the transparency of an instance, select **Alpha** from the **Color** drop-down list. The default setting of **100%** displays the symbol at full opacity. To make the symbol more transparent, move the **Alpha** slider down, or enter a value between **0** and **99** in the **Alpha** field. An **Alpha** setting of **0** makes the instance completely transparent.

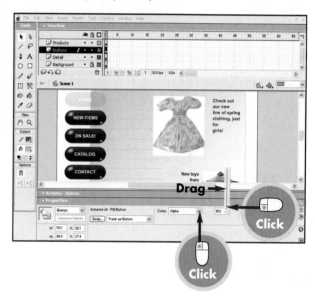

### Animating Brightness, Tint, and Transparency

You can animate the brightness, tint, and transparency effects over time. You'll learn more about this in Part 3, "Basic Animation."

# How to Break Apart Instances

As you learned in Task 5, "How to Edit Symbols," the changes you make in symbol-editing mode affect the master symbol and each instance that links back to it. This could also affect symbols and instances in other movies if you use shared-symbol libraries. To edit an instance without changing the others, you must break the instance apart. This breaks the connection to the original master symbol and allows you to edit it without affecting the master and its other instances. Then, you can convert the new version into a new master symbol. These points are illustrated in the steps that follow.

## 1 Place Several Instances on the Stage

Drag several instances of a symbol from your Library to create multiple copies on the Stage.

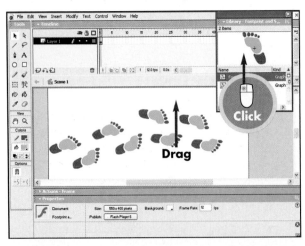

## 2 Select the Instance

Select the **Arrow** tool from the toolbox. Click one of the instances on the Stage to select it.

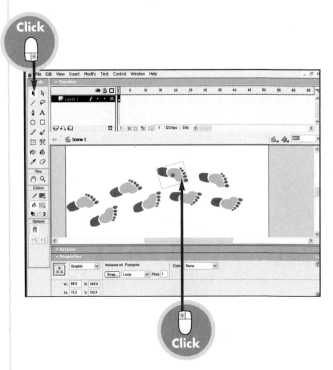

## ③ Apply the Break Apart Command

Select **Modify, Break Apart**, or use the keyboard shortcut (**Option-B**) [**Ctrl+B**]. If the symbol is grouped (see Part 1, Task 6, "How to Create and Group Shapes and Strokes"), you might need to repeat this command more than once until the symbol is completely editable (dotted). Flash breaks apart the symbol and selects all the components that make up the symbol.

## ④ Edit the Objects

The link to the master symbol is now broken, so you can edit the instance without affecting the other instances you placed on the Stage.

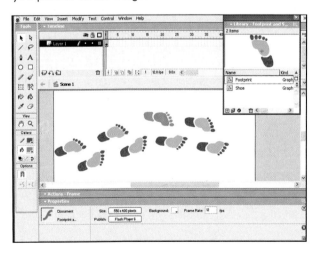

## ⑤ Select the Objects

Use the **Arrow** tool to draw a rectangular selection around all the objects you edited.

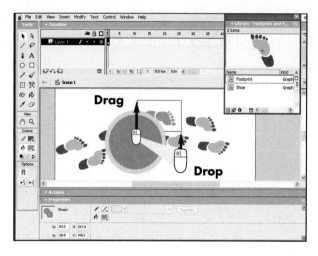

## ⑥ Name the New Symbol

Select **Insert, Convert to Symbol**, or use the keyboard shortcut **F8** to open the **Symbol Properties** dialog box. Enter a new name for the symbol in the **Name** field, and select one of the **Behavior** types (**Graphic, Button**, or **Movie Clip**). Click **OK** to add the new symbol to your movie Library.

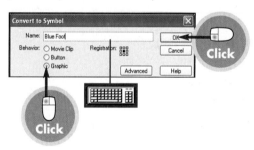

---

How to Hint

## Break Apart with Caution!

Be careful when you break apart symbols—especially symbols that are animated or very complex. For example, when you break apart an animated symbol, Flash discards all frames but the current frame, and your symbol will no longer animate.

# How to Create a Movie Clip

You'll learn about animation in the next part, so this is the perfect time to discuss Movie Clips. A Movie Clip is a very special type of symbol that is somewhat similar to a Flash minimovie in itself. Movie Clips can contain animation, other symbols, text, imported artwork, and interactive buttons. You can place Movie Clips anywhere in your project—the Movie Clip animates independently of the movie, even on a single frame.

## ❶ Create a New Symbol

With nothing selected on the Stage, select **Insert, New Symbol**. The **Symbol Properties** dialog box appears. Enter a name for the symbol in the **Name** field (such as **Clock**, shown here), and select **Movie Clip** for the behavior. Click **OK** to enter symbol-editing mode.

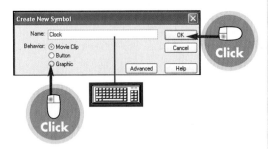

## ❷ Develop Your Frames

If you want to animate your Movie Clip, you must create multiple frames. In the example shown here, the pendulum of the clock swings back and forth through the use of *tweens*, which you'll learn more about in Part 3, "Basic Animation."

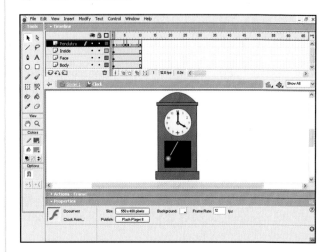

## ③ Add the Movie Clip to Your Main Movie

When your movie clip is complete, select **Edit**, **Document** or click the **Scene** tab (at the left of the Clock tab in this example) to return to movie-editing mode. If necessary, create a new layer for your Movie Clip. Then, click and drag your new symbol from the movie Library onto the new layer.

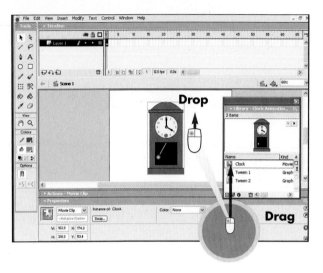

## ④ Test the Movie

Even though this sample movie contains only one frame, the Movie Clip still animates. To view the Movie Clip as it plays in the single frame, select **Control**, **Test Movie**. The movie plays in a new window. Close the new window to return to editing your movie.

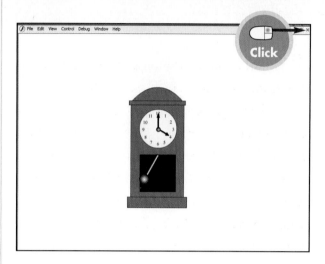

---

**How to Hint**

## Animated Buttons!

Because Movie Clips animate in a single frame, they are ideal for use in creating animated buttons. Use a Movie Clip as the Over state of a button. When your mouse hovers over the button, the button displays an animation. This is covered in Part 5.

Task

**3**

# Basic Animation

**F**lash helps you create impressive animations using a technique called *tweening*. All animation is done by adding frames and keyframes to the timeline. When you create a tween, you create the artwork for the first frame in the animated sequence. Later in the timeframe you add a keyframe and create the artwork for the final frame of the animation sequence. Then, you create a tween that automatically generates all the frames in between the first and last frame (hence, the meaning of the word *tween*).

Tweening enables you to create complex animations in a fraction of the time that it takes to create traditional frame-by-frame animation. They result in smaller file sizes because Flash stores only the values for the actual changes between frames, not the complete set of values for each frame, as with frame-by-frame animation.

There are two types of tweens. A motion tween enables you to change certain properties of a symbol (its size, color, effect, rotation, or position). A shape tween enables you to transform one shape into another. You'll learn how to create both types of tweens in this part.

# How to Use the Timeline

The Timeline is one of the central components you use while creating Flash animations. In the Timeline, you add layers, frames, and keyframes that control where elements, transitions, and sounds appear on the Stage or start playing. You can dock and undock the Timeline to position it in any convenient place. In addition, you can customize how the Timeline displays the frames.

## 1 Undock the Timeline

To undock the Timeline, click in the blank area above the layers list and drag the Timeline to tear it away from the main application window. Release the mouse button to position the Timeline in its own floating window.

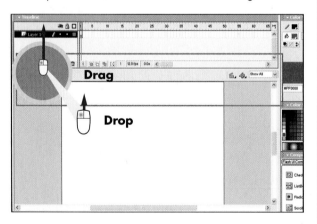

## 2 Redock the Timeline

To redock the Timeline, drag it back to any edge of the application window. The Timeline can be docked to the left, right, top, or bottom of the application window. Release the mouse button to dock the Timeline.

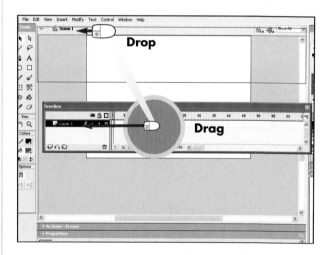

How to Hint

### How to Prevent the Timeline from Redocking

You can move the Timeline over the top of the Stage without redocking it. Simply press the **Ctrl** key while you move the Timeline. To permanently prevent redocking, select **Edit**, **Preferences**, and check the **Disable Timeline Docking** option in the Preferences dialog box.

## ③ View Layers in the Timeline

Click the **Insert Layer** icon or select **Insert**, **Layer** to add as many layers to the Timeline as you like. If you have more layers than can be displayed at one time, use the right Timeline scrollbar to move up and down through the layers list. Click the up and down arrows to move in small increments, or drag the slider up or down to move in larger increments.

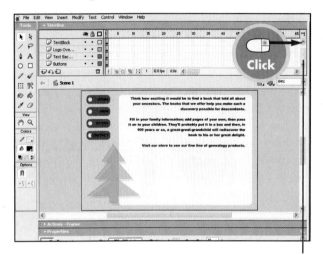

Right scrollbar

## ④ Resize the Timeline

You can also resize the Timeline to display more layers. To resize the Timeline, position the cursor over the bottom edge of the Timeline. When you see a double-arrow cursor, click and drag the bottom edge up or down.

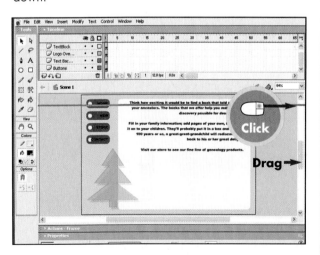

## ⑤ Scroll Through the Timeline

If your animation has more frames than you can see in the Timeline, you can drag the bottom scrollbar left to move backward through your animation, or drag it right to move forward. Click the back and forward arrows to move in increments of five frames at a time.

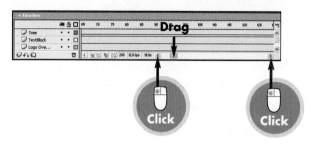

## ⑥ Change the Timeline Frame View

To change the width of the frames in the Timeline, click the **Frame View** button at the right side of the Timeline to open the **Frame View** drop-down list and select a frame size. Select **Preview** to view thumbnail versions of each frame in the Timeline; select **Preview in Context** to view exact thumbnails of the Stage at each frame (including blank areas of the Stage).

Frame View button

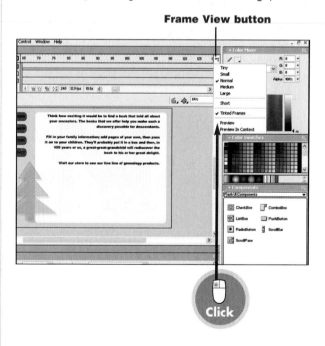

# How to Add Frames and Keyframes

**W**hen you first create a Flash movie, one frame exists in a single layer. To display an object for more than one frame, you need to add more frames. A frame is nothing more than a single segment of your movie—the more frames in your movie, the longer it is. Flash uses three types of frames: regular (or static) frames, keyframes, and blank keyframes. The purposes for these are described in this task.

## ❶ Add Static Frames

To display an object across multiple frames without changing the object, you need to add a regular (or static) frame. After you add an object on the Stage, simply scroll the Timeline until you reach the number of frames you want to display the object. Click the frame on the appropriate layer; then either press **F5** or select **Insert**, **Frame**. The range of static frames appears as a solid bar.

## ❷ Add a Keyframe

When you need to move or change the appearance of an object in a frame or mark the start or end of a *tween* (described later in this part), you add a *keyframe*. To add a keyframe, locate the frame in which you want a change to take place. Click the frame in the appropriate layer, and then either select **Insert**, **Keyframe** or press **F6**. Flash copies the object from the previous frame into the keyframe; then you can change the object as desired.

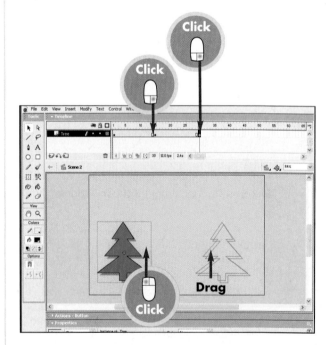

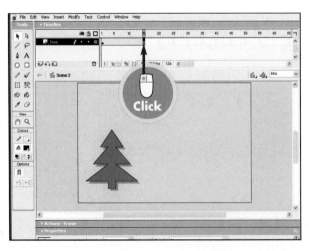

## ③ Add a Blank Keyframe

A blank keyframe removes any content that previously appeared in the frame. From the new keyframe on, that information no longer appears on the Stage. To add a blank keyframe to any frame on any layer, place the cursor in the target frame on the Timeline. Select **Insert**, **Blank Keyframe**. Alternatively, (Ctrl-click) [right-click] the target frame, and select **Insert Blank Keyframe**. Blank keyframes appear as frames with hollow circles.

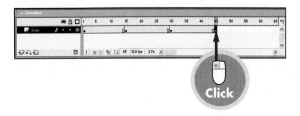

## ④ Clear Keyframes

If you decide you no longer want a change to occur in a specific frame, you can clear the keyframe. Select the keyframe you want to clear, and then select **Insert**, **Clear Keyframe**. You can also use the keyboard shortcut **Shift+F6** or right-click and select **Clear Keyframe**. Flash turns the keyframe into a regular frame and displays the object as dictated by the next earliest keyframe. Your project maintains the same total number of frames.

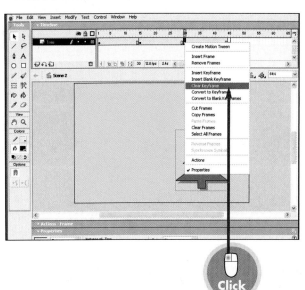

## ⑤ Delete Frames

When you delete frames, you shorten the length of your movie or reduce the amount of time in which changes occur. To delete one or more frames, click (or click and drag) in the Timeline to select the frame(s) you want to delete. Then, select **Insert**, **Remove Frames**; use the keyboard shortcut **Shift+F5**; or right-click the frame and select **Remove Frames**. This removes information from the Stage and deletes the frame. Your project now contains fewer frames.

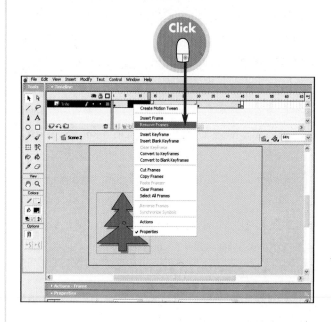

### How to Hint

### More About Frames

If you add a frame or keyframe beyond the last frame of the current layer, Flash adds extra frames to fill in between the first keyframe and the new keyframe. However, if you insert a keyframe on an already existing frame, Flash converts the existing frame to a keyframe without adding frames.

### Deleting Keyframes

If you use the Remove Frames command to delete a keyframe that occurs before the end of a movie, Flash does not remove the keyframe. Instead, it removes a regular frame. To remove a keyframe, you must first use the Clear Keyframe command, and then select the Remove Frame command.

# How to Move Objects

One way to create animation very quickly in Flash is to use *tweens* (short for "in between"). For the most basic tween, you add a keyframe to start the animation. You then add a second keyframe where you want the tween to end and move the object. This is known as a *motion tween*, and you can use it with text, symbols, instances, or a single group of objects. This task shows how to move an object from the left of the Stage into the center of the Stage. The object pauses for a while and then moves off the right side of the Stage at the end.

### 1 Add a Symbol

Create a symbol and add it to your library. Press **F11** to open the library, and drag the symbol into the first frame of a new project. Position the symbol in the work area at the left of the Stage.

### 2 Create the Ending Keyframe

Click in the Timeline at the frame that represents where you want the first tween to end (frame 20, in this example). Select **Insert**, **Keyframe** or press **F6** on your keyboard to add a keyframe at this location. Then click and drag the object to the center of the Stage. Release the mouse when the object is in its new location.

## How to Hint

### Animation Speed

When you create tweened sequences, keep in mind that you can control the speed at which the object moves from its start position to its end position. To do this, adjust the number of frames in the sequence. Fewer frames in the sequence result in a faster-moving object. Obviously, a longer tweened sequence creates a slower-moving animation. You can also adjust the speed of the animation by changing the movie frame rate. If you leave the number of frames constant, a higher frame rate results in a faster-moving animation.

## ❸ Create the Motion Tween

(Ctrl-click) [right-click] anywhere within the range of frames between the two keyframes, and select **Create Motion Tween** from the menu that appears. A solid arrow with a blue background appears between the starting keyframe and ending keyframe. Click and drag (or *scrub*) the playhead to see the text move across the Stage.

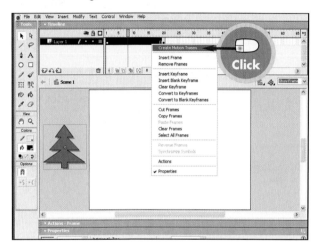

## ❹ Add More Keyframes

Now you'll pause the object until frame 30 and create a second tween that moves the object off the Stage. First, add keyframes (press **F6**) at frames 30 and 50 for the start and end keyframes, respectively. Click frame 50; then move the shape completely off the right side of the Stage.

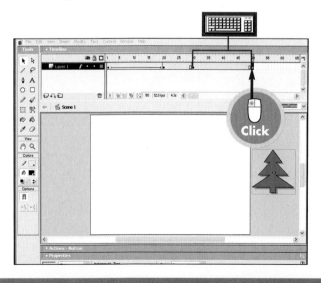

## ❺ Add the Second Motion Tween

Now, right-click any frame between frames 30 and 50, and select **Create Motion Tween** from the menu that appears. Your second tween is complete.

## ❻ Test Your Tweened Sequence

To ensure that your animation performs as you expect it to, click the first frame of the sequence. Select **Control**, **Test Movie** or press (⌘-**Enter**) [**Ctrl+Enter**] to begin playback. If you completed the steps correctly, the object moves smoothly to the center of the Stage, pauses briefly, and then moves off the Stage.

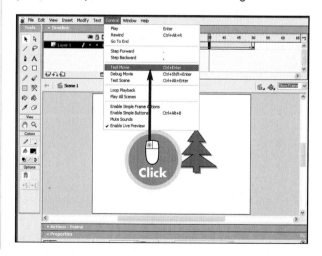

# How to Move Objects Along a Path

In Task 3, "How to Move Objects," you made a tween sequence in which an object moved along a straight line from one position to another. What if you don't want to move the object in a straight line? Flash provides a way for you to move the object along any path you want. This task explains how to accomplish this.

## ① Create a Moving Object

Select **File**, **New** to create a new project. Drag a symbol from your library and place it in frame 1 of Layer 1. Position the object at the desired starting point on the Stage. Next, add a keyframe at frame 20, and move the object to the ending position. Right-click in the Timeline and select **Create Motion Tween**.

## ② Create a Motion Guide Layer

Select the layer that contains the tween you created in step 1; then select **Insert**, **Motion Guide**. Flash creates a new layer directly above the selected layer. Flash automatically names the layer Guide:*name* where *name* represents the name of the layer you clicked. Flash indents the original layer in the layers list to indicate that the Guide layer controls it.

## ③ Create the Motion Path

Select **View**, **Snap to Objects** if object snapping is not enabled. On the Guide layer, click the frame that corresponds to the start of the tween; then use any drawing tool to draw a motion path. Here, a curved path starts and ends at the desired positions on the Stage. Move the object, if necessary, to snap it to the path.

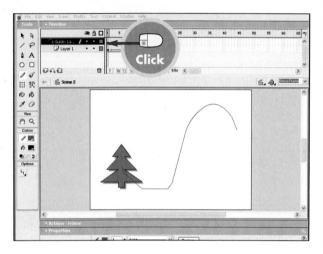

## ④ Snap to the End of the Path

Click the ending keyframe of the object layer to select it, and move the object to a location near the end of the motion path. The object's registration point should snap to the end of the path because you activated snapping in the last step.

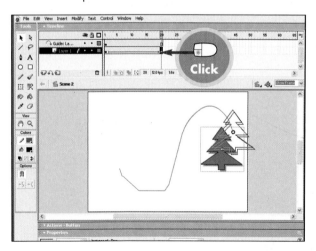

## ⑤ Lock and Hide the Motion Guide

To avoid inadvertently changing your motion guide, lock the Motion Guide layer by clicking the dot under the **Lock** icon. To hide the motion guide so that it does not cause clutter on the Stage during editing, click the black dot under the **Eye** icon.

## ⑥ Test Your Movie

Select **File**, **Save** to save your project because you will continue with it for the next task. Then, select **Control**, **Test Movie** to view your work. You should see the object move along the path as the movie progresses.

# How to Animate Color

Another variation of the motion tween is the Color tween, which changes the color of an object over the course of time. This task shows you how to achieve this effect. At the same time, you'll learn how to create more than one tween by using the same keyframes. Here, you'll continue with the movie you created in the previous task and change the color of the object as it moves across the Stage.

## 1 Create or Select the Starting Keyframe

Create a starting keyframe for the object as outlined previously and add the associated artwork, or click to select an existing keyframe to begin a tween. For this example, use the keyframe that already exists at frame 1 of the shape's layer.

## 2 Create the Ending Keyframe

Similarly, create an ending keyframe and make the desired changes, or click to select an existing ending keyframe. For this example, use the keyframe that already exists at frame 20 of the shape's layer.

## ③ Select Tint from the Effect Panel

With the ending keyframe selected, open the Properties window (select **Window**, **Properties**). Then click to select the object you want to change. From the **Color** drop-down list in the Properties window, select the color property you want to change. For this example, select **Tint** from the list.

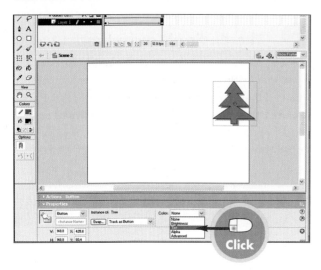

## ④ Select a New Instance Color

The Tint options in the Properties window allow you to select a new color and control the amount of tint to apply to the object. Click the **Tint Color** chooser box, drag through the colors in the current palette, and release the mouse when you find a color you like. Click and drag the **Percentage** slider to vary the amount of tint applied to the instance.

## ⑤ Create the Tween

In the example shown here, we have used an existing motion tween to change the color at the same time that the object moves across the screen. If a motion tween does not already exist, create one now. (Ctrl-click) [right-click] in the span of frames between the beginning and ending keyframes; then, select **Create Motion Tween** from the menu that appears.

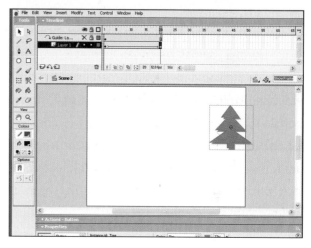

## ⑥ Save the File and Test the Tween

Save your file so that you can continue with the next task. To test the tween, click the first keyframe of the sequence and either select **Control**, **Play** or press (**Return**) [**Enter**] to view the tweened color change.

# How to Fade an Object In or Out

**Y**ou are already beginning to learn that you can use the same tween to achieve multiple effects. Now you'll revise the tween from the previous step so that the object fades out as it moves across the screen. The steps to fade an object in or out are similar to those you use to create a color tween, except that you select the Alpha option from the Color drop-down list. To create a fade-in, set the starting alpha value at 0% and the ending value at 100%. To create a fade-out, set the starting alpha value at 100% and the ending alpha value at 0%.

## ❶ The Starting Keyframe

If a keyframe does not already exist in the frame at which you want a tween to begin, use the steps outlined in previous tasks to add a keyframe and associated artwork. For this example, we'll use the keyframe that already exists at frame 1 of the object layer.

## ❷ The Ending Keyframe

Similarly, if a keyframe does not already exist in the frame at which you want the tween to end, click the frame in the Timeline that you want as the end of your tweened sequence and add another keyframe as outlined in previous tasks. For this example, we will use the keyframe that already exists at frame 20 of the Text layer.

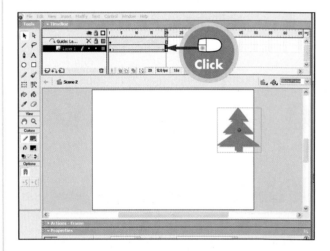

### ③ Select the Alpha Tween Option

Open the **Properties** window if it is not already open. Click to select the last keyframe of the sequence (frame 20 in this case); then, click the object on the Stage. From the **Color** drop-down list in the Properties window, select **Alpha**.

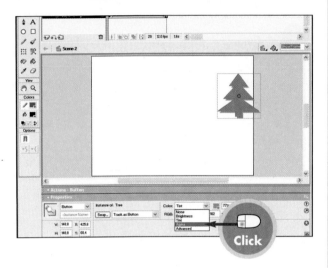

### ④ To Create a Fade-In

If you want to create a fade-in for this tween, click the starting keyframe, select the object, and select **Alpha** from the **Color** drop-down list. Set the starting alpha value at **0%**. Repeat the process to set the alpha value for the ending keyframe to **100%**.

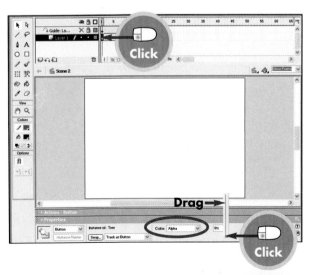

### ⑤ To Create a Fade-Out

If you want to create a fade-out, the starting keyframe should already be 100% alpha (fully opaque) if you did not create the fade-in. Click the ending keyframe, select the object, and select **Alpha** from the drop-down list. Set the ending alpha value to **0%**.

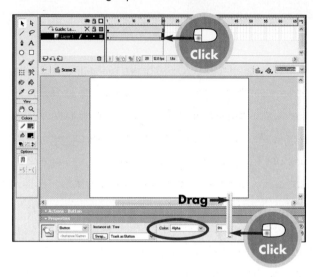

### ⑥ Create the Tween and Test

In the example shown here, we used an existing motion tween to change the alpha. If a motion tween does not already exist, right-click (Ctrl-click on the Mac) in the span of frames between the beginning and ending keyframes and select **Create Motion Tween** from the menu that appears. Finally, click the first keyframe of the sequence, and either select **Control**, **Play** or press (**Return**) [**Enter**] to view the tweened color change.

# How to Zoom Objects In or Out

**S**ize tweens help you achieve several animation effects. When you tween an object equally in both the horizontal and vertical directions, the object appears to fly toward or away from the viewer (as you will learn in this task). If you tween the vertical measurement, you can give the illusion of an object shrinking or growing taller. If you tween only the horizontal measurement, you portray something growing fatter or thinner.

**1** **Create the Starting Keyframe**

Click in the frame at which you want the animation to begin. If a keyframe does not already exist in that frame, select **Insert**, **Keyframe** or use the keyboard shortcut **F6**. Select the new keyframe; then, click and drag a symbol from the Library to the Stage.

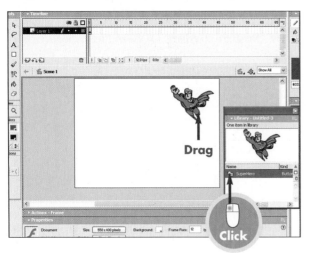

**2** **Create the Ending Keyframe**

Click the frame in the Timeline that you want as the end of your tweened sequence. Select **Insert**, **Keyframe** or press **F6** to add the ending keyframe.

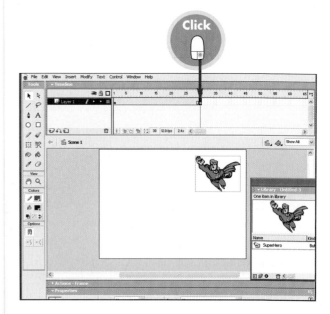

## Scaling by Exact Values

You can use the Transform panel to scale an object by entering numerical values. To open the Transform panel, select **Window**, **Transform**, or use the keyboard shortcut (⌘-**T**) [**Ctrl+T**]. Select the object you want to scale. To scale proportionately, check the **Constrain** option and enter a percentage in either the horizontal or vertical field. To scale disproportionately, uncheck the **Constrain** option and enter different values in the horizontal and vertical fields.

## ③ Scale the Object

Click to select the end keyframe on the appropriate layer. With the object you want to scale selected, either select **Modify**, **Transform**, **Scale** or select the **Free Transform** tool from the **Tools** panel. The object now contains several handles. Shift-click and drag a corner handle to scale an object uniformly; click and drag the top or bottom handle to scale vertically; and click and drag a side handle to scale horizontally.

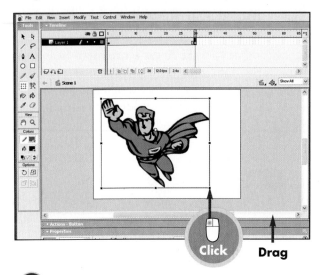

Click     Drag

## ④ Create the Tween

(Ctrl-click) [right-click] in the span of frames between the two keyframes, and select **Create Motion Tween** from the menu that appears.

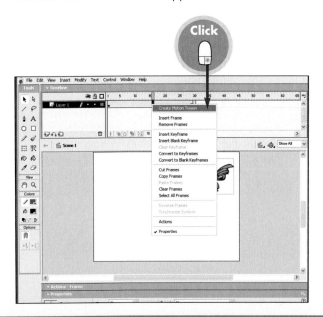

Click

## ⑤ Select the Scaling Option

Select **Window**, **Properties** to open the Properties panel if it is not open. Click anywhere inside the tween to view its properties. For this task, verify that the Scale option is checked. This causes the object to grow gradually during the course of the tweened sequence. Uncheck this box to maintain the object at the same size until the movie enters the final frame of the sequence.

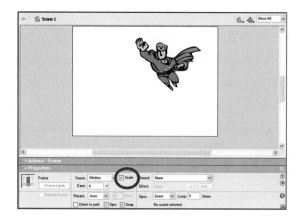

## ⑥ Test Your Tweened Sequence

Click the first keyframe of your sequence, and either select **Control**, **Play** or press (**Return**) [**Enter**] to play the movie. The object should grow or shrink based on how you scaled your object in the end frame.

Click

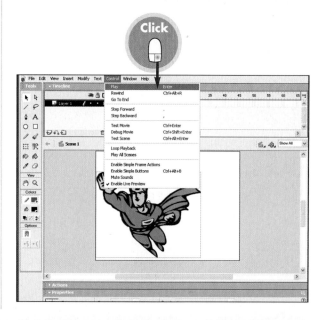

# How to Rotate Objects

This task demonstrates how you create a tweened sequence that rotates a pendulum symbol on the Stage. By default, Flash rotates a symbol around a center transformation point. However, you can adjust the point at which an object rotates. Both techniques are discussed in this task, which shows how you can rotate a pendulum on a clock. Note that you must convert an object into a symbol before you can apply the transformation to it.

## 1 Review the Requirements

Notice that the clock and hands in this example use 30 frames on the Timeline. At the rate of 15 frames per second, we want the pendulum to swing to the right in one second and then to the left in another second. However, by default, the transformation point is in the center of an object. This causes the pendulum to rotate in an unnatural manner.

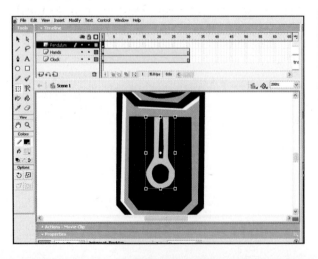

## 2 Move the Registration Point

To move the transformation point to the top center of the pendulum, first click the **Free Transform** tool in the Tools panel. Then drag the transformation point (the white circle) from the center of the object to the top center of the object. Now the pendulum will rotate correctly.

---

### How to Hint

### Rotating by Exact Values

The Transform panel enables you to rotate an object by entering numerical values. Select **Window**, **Transform**, or use the keyboard shortcut (⌘-**T**) [**Ctrl+T**] to open the Transform panel. Select the object you want to rotate, and click the **Rotate** radio button. Enter a positive (clockwise) or negative (counterclockwise) number to rotate the object.

---

### ③ Create the Start Keyframe

Click the frame in the Timeline at which you want your tweened sequence to start. If a keyframe does not already exist, select **Insert, Keyframe** or press **F6** to add one. Hover the **Free Transform** tool near the lower-right corner of the pendulum until you see a Rotate cursor; then rotate the pendulum to the left position.

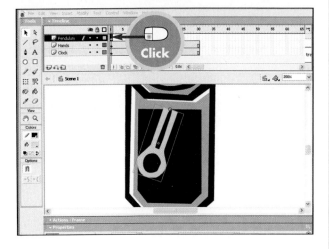

### ④ Complete the First Motion Tween

Click frame 15 in the Pendulum layer and press **F6** to add a keyframe. Select the **Free Transform** tool and verify that the transformation point is at the top center of the pendulum; then, use the Free Transform tool to rotate the pendulum to the right position. Right-click between the two keyframes and select **Create Motion Tween**. The first tween is now complete.

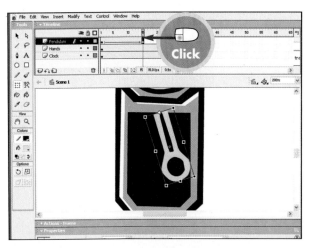

### ⑤ Add the Final Keyframe and Tween

Click frame 30 in the Pendulum layer and press **F6** to add a keyframe. Select the **Free Transform** tool and verify that the transformation point is at the top center of the pendulum. Use the Free Transform tool to rotate the pendulum back to the left position. Then right-click between the two keyframes and select **Create Motion Tween**. The second tween is now complete.

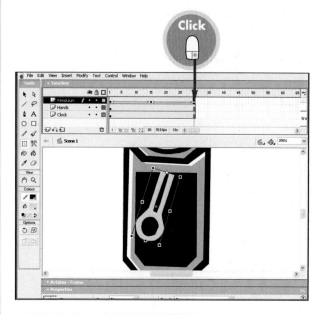

### ⑥ Test Your Tweened Sequence

To view the tween in a loop, click the first keyframe of your sequence and select **Control, Loop Playback**. Then, either select **Control, Play** or press (**Return**) [**Enter**] to play the movie. You should see the pendulum swing from left to right and back again in a loop.

# How to Morph Text

Flash enables you to morph one shape into another. For example, you can morph a square into a circle or one string of text into another string over time. To accomplish this with text, you must break apart the text in the starting and ending keyframes. Afterward, you can apply a shape tween. This task explains how to morph text.

## 1 Create a Keyframe

Create a new project, and select the first frame in Layer 1. Use the Text tool to create a brief text block on the Stage. Then, select **Modify**, **Break Apart** twice to turn the text block into objects.

## 2 Create the Ending Keyframe

Add another keyframe (press **F6**) in frame 20 of the text layer. Delete the existing text, and enter a new string of text. Again, select **Modify**, **Break Apart** twice to turn the new text block into objects.

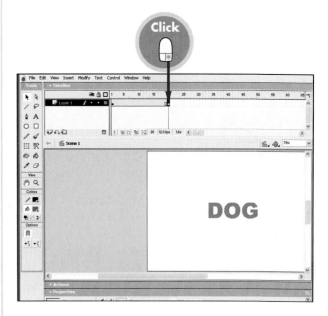

## ③ Open the Properties Window

If the Properties window is not already open, select **Window**, **Properties** to open it.

## ④ Create a Shape Tween

Click anywhere between the first and last keyframes in the Timeline. Then select **Shape** from the **Tween** menu in the Properties window. The shape tween is represented as a series of green frames, with a solid arrow that runs between the keyframes.

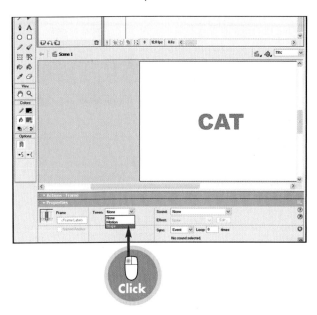

## ⑤ Rewind the Movie

Click the first frame in the Timeline to go to the first frame in the movie, or select **Control**, **Rewind**.

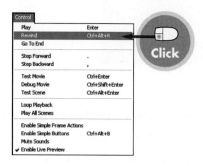

## ⑥ Test the Movie

Select **Control**, **Play** or press (**Return**) [**Enter**] to test the shape tween. You should see one word morph into the other.

How to Hint

## Broken Shape Tweens

If the arrow in the shape tween appears as a dotted line, the tween is broken. One reason for this is that the text might still be grouped. Be sure you break the text apart in both the starting and ending frames before you create the tween.

## Using Shape Hints

You can use shape hints to control the manner in which Flash renders the in-between frames of the letters. For a complete explanation on using shape hints, search for the help topic "Using Shape Hints" in the Macromedia Flash MX help file.

# How to Use Masks

Flash enables you to use masks to create interesting effects. For example, you can use a mask to create a spotlight that moves around the Stage, or you can make a character run behind a pole but not come out at the other side. You can also use it to create interesting fades and wipes, as you'll learn here.

## 1 Create a New Document

Create a new document (**File**, **New**) and keep the dimensions at the default 550 pixels wide and 400 pixels high. Then select **Insert**, **New Symbol**. When the Create New Symbol dialog appears, name the symbol **Wipe**, and select **Movie Clip** as the symbol type.

## 2 Create a Mask Shape

Select the **Rectangle** tool from the Tools palette. Select black for a fill color, and turn off the stroke color.

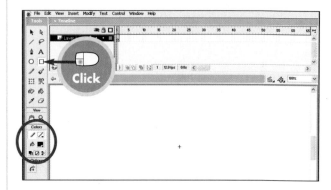

## 3 Draw a Rectangle

Draw a rectangle. Click it with the **Arrow** tool, and enter precise measurements and coordinates in the **W**, **H**, **X**, and **Y** fields in the Properties window: **55** pixels for W, **400** pixels for H, **-28** (half of the width) for X, and **-200** (half of the height) for Y. This centers the rectangle around the registration point.

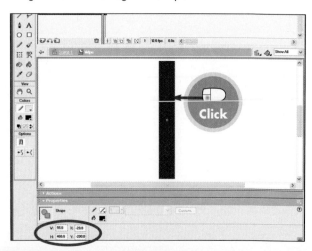

## ④ Convert the Rectangle to a Symbol

Select the rectangle and select **Insert**, **Convert to Symbol** (**F8**). Name the symbol `Rectangle`, and select **Graphic** as the symbol type.

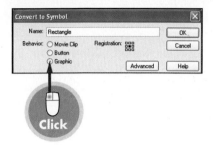

## ④ Add a Keyframe and Adjust the Rectangle

Add a keyframe (**F6**) at frame 20. Click the **Free Transform** tool in the toolbox, and use the fields in the Properties window to resize and reposition the rectangle as follows: Set the width to 1 pixel, and move the X position to 0 so that the rectangle moves over the registration point.

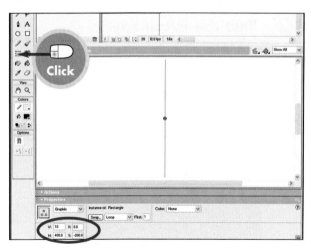

## ⑤ Create a Tween

Click anywhere between the two frames in the Timeline, and select **Insert**, **Create Motion Tween**. Scrub through the Timeline to ensure that the tween works. You should see it gradually narrowing in width, and it should remain centered around the registration point.

## ⑥ Create a Background

Select **Edit**, **Edit Document** to return to the Stage. Now, create any type of background you want. If you want to keep it simple, use a solid color. Here, the background consists of two layers: a forest layer and a gradient rectangle. The mask can affect one or both of these layers with the wipe.

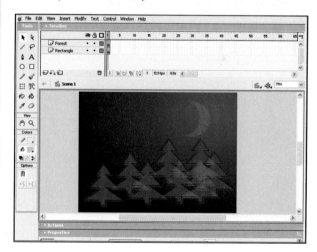

## ⑦ Add the First Wipe Symbol

Highlight the layer you want to mask (in this case, the Forest layer). Create a new layer and name it **Wipe**. Drag a copy of the Wipe symbol from the library and place it on the Stage. In the Properties window, enter **0** for an X coordinate and **0** for a Y coordinate. This places the first rectangle at the edge of the Stage.

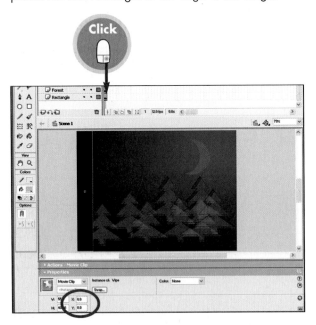

## ⑧ Add the Remaining Wipe Symbols

Create nine copies of the Wipe symbol by (Option-clicking) [Alt-clicking], copying and pasting to and from the Clipboard, or dragging them from the Library. The remaining symbols will use Y coordinates of 0, but the X coordinates will be set at 55, 110, 165, 220, 275, 330, 385, 440, and 495, respectively. Select all 10 wipes, and select **Insert**, **Convert to Symbol** to convert them to a single movie clip called FullWipe.

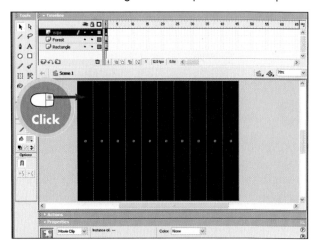

## ⑨ Test the Wipe Layer

Because the Wipe symbols are movie clips, they play independently of the main Timeline. To view the animated wipe symbols, select **Control**, **Test Movie**. You should see the Stage start out as black and gradually give way to the background image. Select **File**, **Close** from the preview window to return to the Stage.

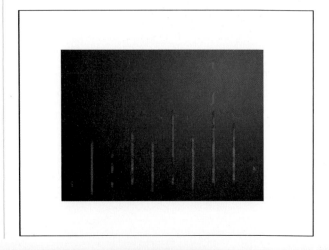

## 10  Create the Mask Layer

Select the Wipe layer. Right-click and select **Mask** from the menu that appears. The Wipe layer turns into a mask layer and automatically masks the layer below it. Flash automatically locks the two layers so that you can't edit them further. Now, when you test the movie, you will see the mask gradually remove the masked layer from the screen to reveal the background.

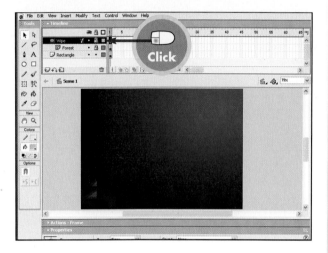

## 11  Mask Additional Layers

Assume that you want to remove the blue gradient and the Forest layer from this scene and reveal the movie background color. It's easy—simply drag the Background layer and place it beneath the Forest layer, which is already under control of the mask.

## 12  Retest the Movie

With both layers under control of the mask, select **Control**, **Test Movie** again. Now, the mask gradually removes both the blue gradient layer and the Forest layer. Again, select **File**, **Close** to return to the Stage.

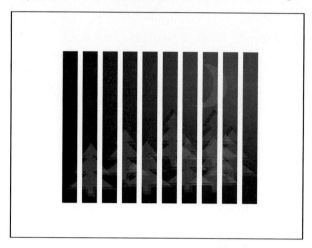

## 13  Continue the Movie

Now you can create additional content for the movie. Add another layer above the mask layer. Then select the mask layer, and drag it and its children on top of the new layer. Return to the new layer and add more content, making it as long as you like. The wipe will play only once.

Task

# Advanced Animation

**A**dvanced animation, such as frame-by-frame animation, is a little more involved than tweened animation because you are doing more of the work yourself instead of having Flash do a bulk of the work for you. However, as you'll learn in this part, Flash provides some tools that help you develop and manage your movies more easily. Flash's onion skin feature mimics the onion skinning of traditional animation and allows you to view before and after frames while you focus on drawing the in-between frames. Tweens help you create scrolling backgrounds that enable you to focus your animation in the center of the Stage. And scenes help break your movies into manageable chunks. You'll learn about all these features in this part.

# How to Use Onion Skinning

**W**hen you create a frame-by-frame animation, it helps to use onion skinning. Basically, the onion skinning feature of Flash enables you to view partially transparent images of the frames immediately before and after your current frame, so that you can draw the in-between frames accurately. In the following task, you'll step through each onion skin feature. If you want to work with a file as you display the onion skin, create a simple 20-frame tweened animation using one of the methods outlined in Part 3, "Basic Animation."

### 1 Turn Onion Skin On or Off

To turn onion skinning on and off, click the **Onion Skin** icon below the Timeline. The icon is pressed inward when onion skinning is on. By default, onion skinning displays three frames.

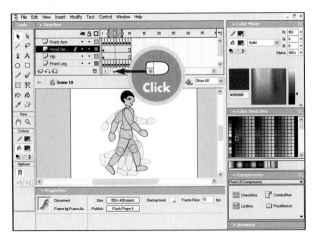

### 2 Center on the Current Frame

To center the Timeline on the current frame, click the **Center Frame** icon below the Timeline.

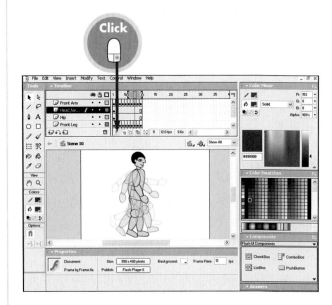

## ③ Turn On Outlines

To display onion-skinned frames as outlines, click the **Onion Skin Outlines** icon below the Timeline. The current frame appears solid. Flash uses the layer color (shown in the color squares in the layer list) to display the onion-skinned frames. Frames that are outside the onion markers do not display.

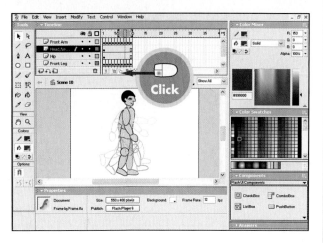

## ⑤ View the Onion Markers Menu

The fifth icon below the Timeline is the Onion Markers menu, which allows you to change the display of the onion markers above the Timeline. Click the **Onion Markers** menu to display the choices that are described in the following steps.

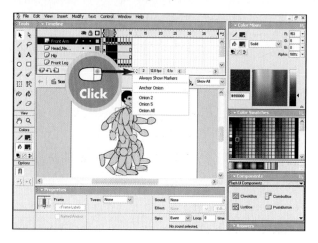

## ④ Edit Multiple Frames

To edit more than one frame at a time, click the **Edit Multiple Frames** icon below the Timeline. In this mode, you can select any set of objects in a single frame or in a range of frames for editing.

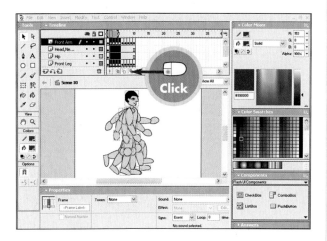

## ⑥ Display Onion Markers Permanently

You can display the onion markers above the Timeline at all times, whether or not you have Onion Skinning turned on. To do so, select the **Always Show Markers** command from the **Onion Markers** menu.

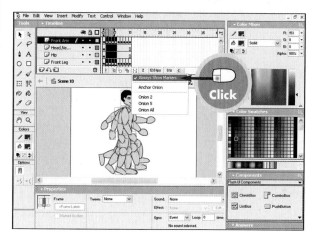

## **7** Lock the Onion Markers

Normally, the onion markers move around the frame that is currently selected. To lock the onion markers in a fixed position, select **Anchor Onion** from the **Onion Markers** menu. The onion markers remain in the same position regardless of which frame you are currently editing.

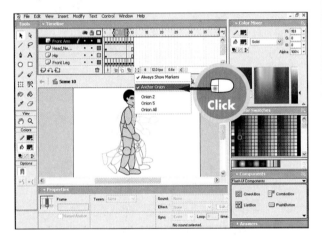

## **8** Show Onion Skinning for 5 Frames

To onion skin two frames before and two frames after the current frame, select **Onion 2** from the **Onion Markers** menu.

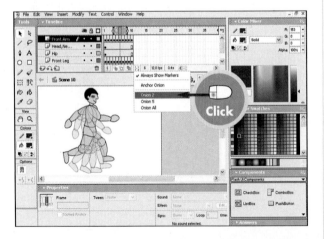

## **9** Show Onion Skinning for 11 Frames

To display onion skinning for 11 frames, starting 5 frames before the current frame and ending 5 frames after the current frame, select **Onion 5** from the **Onion Markers** menu.

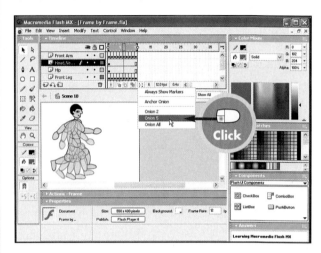

## **10** Show Onion Skinning for All Frames

To display onion skinning for all frames, select **Onion All** from the **Onion Markers** menu. You'll probably find this most helpful to track the movement of a single layer throughout the entire animation. You can hide the layers you do not want to display in onion skin mode.

**Hidden layer**

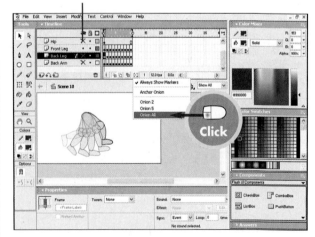

## 11 Show Onion Skinning for Any Number of Frames

To display onion skinning for the frames you want to view, position the onion markers at the center frame. Drag the starting and ending markers left or right so that the onion markers begin and end at the frames you want to view.

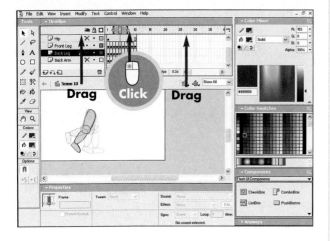

## 12 Moving or Rescaling an Animation

Onion skinning also helps you move or rescale the contents of the entire animation at once. To do so, make sure that all layers are unlocked. Then, click the **Show Multiple Frames** button in the Timeline and use the onion markers to enclose the range of frames you want to move (any or all of them).

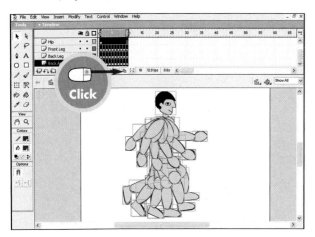

## 13 Move, Scale, or Rotate the Selection

After you enclose and select the frames, you can move them to another location on the Stage. You can also use commands in the **Modify, Transform** command list to scale or rotate the entire selection at once.

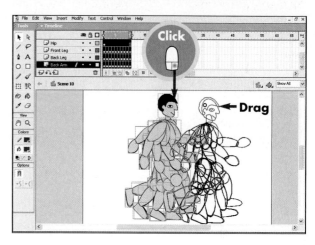

How to Hint

## Locking Layers

When editing multiple frames, as described in step 4, you should lock layers that you do not want to change inadvertently. To lock the items in a layer, simply click the dot in the **Padlock** column. The dot turns into a Padlock icon when the layer is locked. Flash still displays locked layers but does not allow you to change them.

## Hiding Layers

Onion skinning can sometimes get very confusing if too many layers are displayed. To cut down on the amount of information that appears in onion skin mode, simply hide the layers you don't want to view. Click the dot in the **Eye** column for each layer in the layer list that you want to hide, as shown in Step 10.

# How to Create a Scrolling Background

**S**crolling backgrounds are often used in cartoon animation. For example, when a character is walking or running across the screen (as shown in the previous task), the character stays in the center of the Stage while the background moves behind the character. In this project, you'll use a background image that is the same size as the movie (500×400 pixels), and you'll scroll the background horizontally. Two copies of the background image are required, and you need to place them side by side. For this reason, the images must match at the right and left sides (for horizontal scrolling) or at the top and bottom (for vertical scrolling).

## ❶ Backgrounds for Horizontal Scrolling

When you design a background image that scrolls horizontally, such as when a character is walking toward the right or left of the Stage (as shown here), or from left to right (as shown in Project 1), the left and right edges of your image should match when placed next to each other, as shown here.

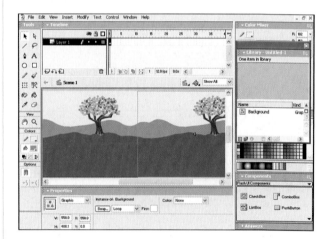

## ② Backgrounds for Vertical Scrolling

When you design a background image that scrolls vertically, such as when a plane is flying over a runway, the top and bottom edges should match when placed next to each other, as shown here (a slight space appears intentionally between the two images so you can see the seam).

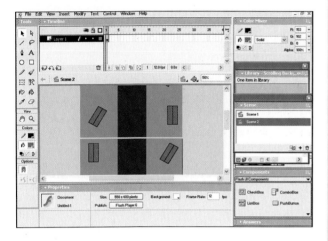

## ③ Create a New Movie

Select **File, New** or use the shortcut (⌘**+N**) or [**Ctrl+N**] to create a new 550×400 pixel movie. Create or import a 550×400 pixel background image, placing it so that it completely covers the stage. Convert it into a graphic symbol (**F8**) so that it appears in the project library.

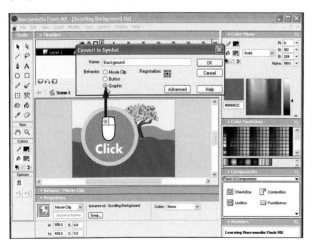

## ④ Create a New Symbol

Select the background instance on the stage, and select **Insert, Convert to Symbol** again (**F8** for Mac and Windows). Name the symbol **Scrolling Background** and select the **Movie Clip** behavior. Double-click the Stage to enter symbol-editing mode, where the background image appears in the center of the Stage.

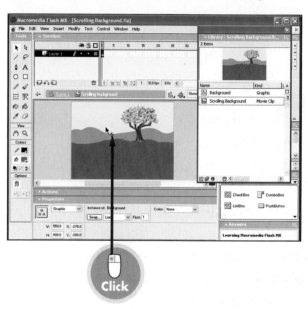

## ⑤ Create a Keyframe

While in symbol-editing mode for the scrolling background symbol, click to select frame 20 and insert a keyframe (**F6**) in Layer 1.

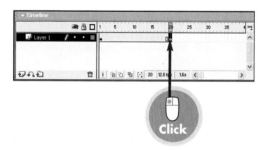

## ⑥ Move the Background Off the Stage

Zoom out so that you can see the work area around the Stage. Then drag the first background so that it is 1 pixel to the right of the movie Stage. For example, if your dimensions are 550 by 400, the X coordinate in the Properties window should be at 275, as shown here.

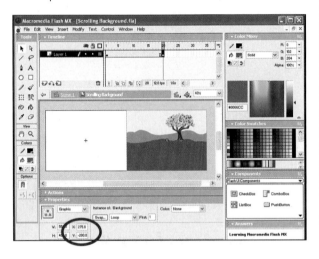

## ⑦ Create a Motion Tween

Click in the first frame and select **Insert, Create Motion Tween**. This creates a tween that moves the background off the Stage from frame 0 to frame 20.

## ⑧ Create a Second Layer

Now you'll add a second layer to the scrolling background symbol. While still in symbol-editing mode, click the **Insert Layer** button at the lower-left corner of the Timeline layer list.

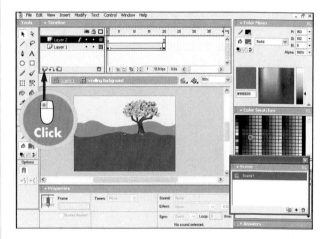

## ⑨ Add a Second Background Copy

Drag and drop a second copy of your background image from the movie library and place it at the left of the Stage, with the right end of the background image on the new layer butted against the left end of the background image on the first layer. (the x, y coordinate in the Properties window should be −825, −200). Flash automatically adds a keyframe to the first frame and adds frames for the remainder of the layer.

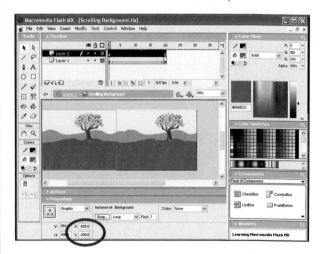

## 10 Move the Second Symbol

Insert a keyframe (**F6**) in frame 20 of the second layer. With frame 20 selected, move the background symbol in the second layer so that it completely covers the Stage. The right end of the background should butt up against the left end of the symbol on the first layer. In this example, the x, y coordinate is –275, –200.

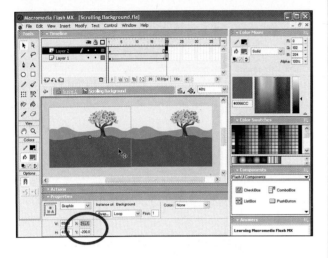

## 11 Complete the Tween

Click in the first frame of the second layer and select **Insert, Create Motion Tween**. This creates a tween that moves Layer 2 from the left of the Stage to center Stage from frame 0 to frame 20.

## 12 Test Your Movie

Now, exit symbol-editing mode and return to the main movie. The movie clip is a separate animation in itself on the first frame. To test your movie, select **Control, Test Movie** (⌘-**Enter**) [**Ctrl+Enter**]. The preview might give the impression that the animation does not play correctly between the last and first frames; however, when you publish the movie the scrolling will be smooth.

**Click to close preview**

## 13 Add Movie Foreground Layers

Close the preview window and return to the movie. Now you can add movie clips or animations in layers above the scrolling background. The background movie clip will scroll through the length of the entire animation.

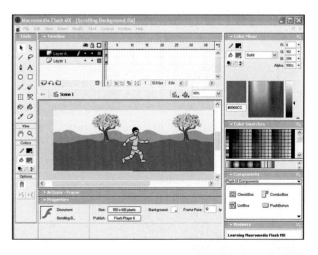

**③**

# How to Add Another Scene

**A** movie can contain multiple scenes that help divide it into smaller, more manageable chunks. Scenes can also display background changes or entirely different content. The Scene panel helps you create, delete, and manage the scenes in your Flash movie. Flash plays the scenes in the order in which they appear in the Scene panel. The movie progresses from one scene to the next automatically, unless a scene contains a Stop action that prevents this from occurring. This task helps illustrate these points.

**①  Open the Scene Panel**

To open the Scene panel, select **Window, Scene**, or use the keyboard shortcut **Shift+F2**.

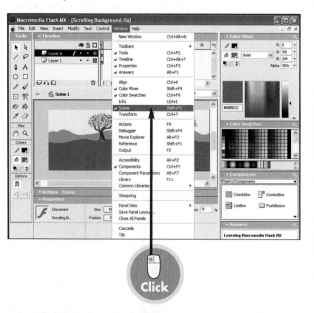

**②  Add Another Scene**

Click the **Add Scene** button at the bottom of the Scene panel. Double-click the scene name to rename the scene appropriately. (For this example, name it **Paused Background**.)

## 3 Continue a Scrolling Background

In the preceding task, you created a scrolling background. Suppose that in the scene you just created, you want to stop the scrolling for a while and then resume it again after some animation is complete. Using this as an example, rename the Paused Background Layer 1 to **Background**. Drag the original background symbol from the library (the symbol or bitmap from which you created the scrolling background) and place it on the Stage.

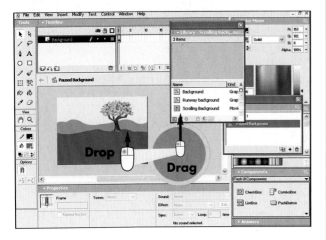

## 4 Add Animated Content

Create additional layers above the background layer to add your animated content. Add a keyframe in the final frame of the background layer so that the background remains still throughout the entire animation.

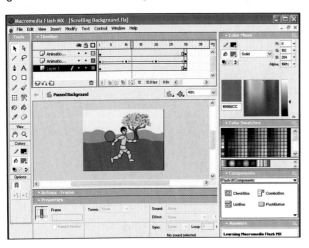

## 5 Restart the Scrolling Background

To restart the scrolling background in the next scene, select the **Paused Background** scene and click the **Add Scene** button. Name this scene **Resume Scrolling** and place it third in the list. In the Timeline, rename Layer 1 to **Scrolling Background** and place the Scrolling Background symbol into the first frame. Add additional animated layers above the background layer as needed.

## 6 Duplicate an Existing Scene

If you want to create a scene that is an exact or near exact duplicate of an existing scene, select the scene you want to duplicate. Then, click the **Duplicate Scene** button in the Scene panel. Flash places the duplicate copy immediately beneath the scene you selected.

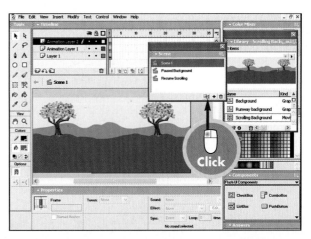

# How to Create Frame-by-Frame Animation

**F**rame-by-frame animation is not as complicated as you might think, especially with the tools you have at hand with Flash. Although it's common to draw the changes in each frame by hand, you can also accomplish quite a lot by developing several symbols that you can move, rotate, and resize as you develop your frame-by-frame animation. A good way to learn frame-by-frame animation is to create a walk cycle for a character. First, you'll create several body parts for the character, as simple or as detailed as you like. Then, you'll use Flash's onion-skin feature to position the various body parts to create a smooth animation.

## ❶ Create a New Movie

Select **File**, **New** to create a new movie with the default settings.

## ❷ Create the Body Parts

Use Flash's drawing tools to create several body parts. Place the head and neck on Layer 1 and rename the layer to Head. Add additional layers for the torso, the upper arm, the lower arm, the upper legs, and the lower legs, respectively. Later, you'll use each of the arm and leg symbols twice.

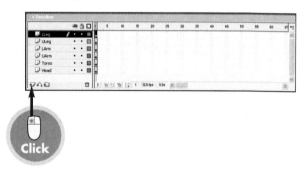

## ❸ Convert the Parts to Symbols

To convert all the body parts to symbols, select each body part one at a time, and select **Insert**, **Convert to Symbol**. Name the part appropriately, and select the **Graphic** symbol type.

## ④ Duplicate the Arms and Legs

Select the upper arm part and copy it to the clipboard (**Edit**, **Copy**). Then create a new layer and name it Upper Arm. Select **Edit**, **Paste** to paste the upper arm in the new layer. Repeat this process for the remaining arm and leg parts, using layer names that relate to each part.

## ⑤ Reorder the Layers

Reorder the layers in the Timeline so that they appear as follows from the top of the list to the bottom: LowerArm1, UpperArm1, LowerLeg1, and LowerLeg2 (the front limbs); LowerLeg2 and UpperLeg2 (the back leg); Torso; LowerArm2 and UpperArm2 (the back arm); and Head. As you layer the parts, place them in their correct positions to build your character.

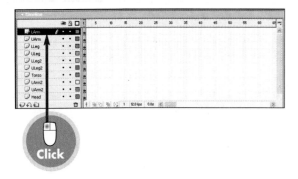

## ⑥ Rescale the Character

If necessary, use the Arrow tool to draw a rectangular selection around all the body parts on the Stage. Then select the **Free Transform** tool and resize the character so that it fits well on the Stage.

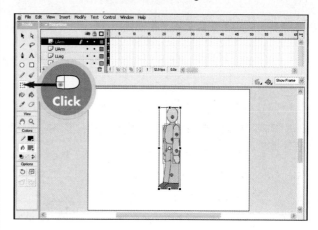

## ⑦ Rotate the Parts

Now use the Free Transform tool to move and rotate each of the limb parts to achieve your starting position. About the only thing to remember at this point is that the opposite leg and arm move from front to back at the same time (for example, when the right arm is in front, the left leg is in front). An example is shown here.

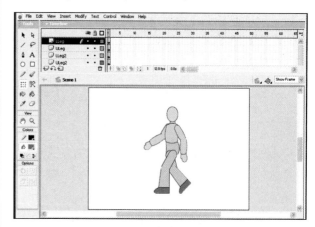

## ⑧ Turn on Onion Skinning

Click the **Onion Skin** button to turn on the Onion Skin feature. The Onion Skin indicator appears at the top of the Timeline. The remaining part of the process is simply to move and rotate the body parts in each individual frame until you complete the walk cycle. As you do so, the Onion Skin feature helps you gauge where to position and rotate the part to achieve a smooth animation.

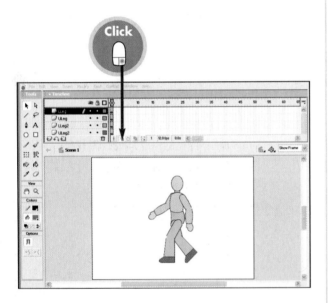

## ⑨ Add Frames for the Head and Torso

In this example, you will keep the head and torso stationary throughout the animation. To see them on every frame, you need to place a regular frame in what will be the last frame of the walk cycle. Click the last frame in the head and torso layers and press **F5** to extend the layers to the length of the animation (10 frames, in this case).

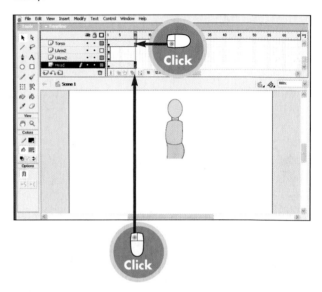

## ⑩ Add Keyframes

Select the second frame in the Timeline, and add keyframes (**F6**) for each of the remaining body parts. When you add each keyframe, Flash copies the limb from the first frame into the new frame. When you're done, all the limbs should be visible on the Stage.

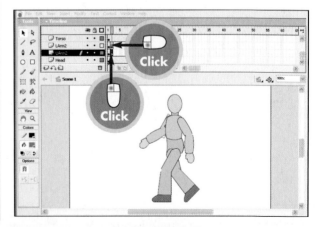

## 11 Plan the Motion

To create a complete walk cycle in 10 frames, you must move one pair of limbs from front to back in the first 5 frames, and then from back to front until you almost reach the starting position in frame 10. The opposite pair of limbs moves in the opposite direction.

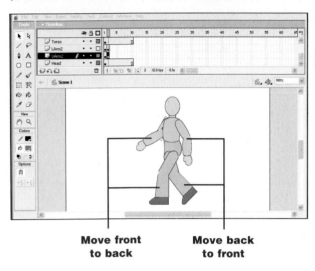

**Move front to back**  **Move back to front**

## 12 View the Changes

As you move the body parts, you might find it easier to show or hide layers or view the Stage in outline mode. To hide layers, click the eye icon that corresponds to a layer. Click the icon again to unhide the layer. To view the Stage in outline mode, click the **Onion Skin Outlines** button located beneath the Timeline. The current frame appears solid, whereas the adjacent frames appear semitransparent.

**Click to show or hide layers**  **Click to view in outline mode**

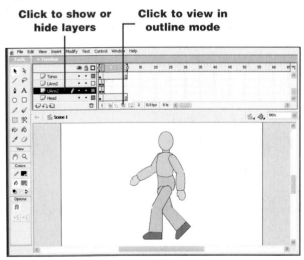

## 13 Start the Second Frame

Select one of the body parts, such as the front upper arm. Move the transformation point, if necessary, as discussed in Part 3, Task 8, "How to Rotate Objects." Then with the **Free Transform** tool, rotate the body part so that it moves about one-fifth of the way toward the opposite direction.

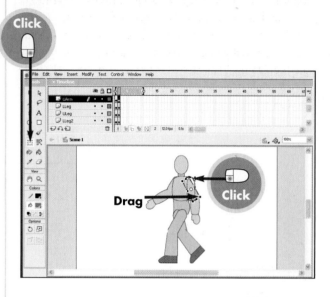

**Click**  **Drag**  **Click**

## 14 Move the Arm into Place

After you rotate the arm, move it into the correct position at the shoulder if necessary.

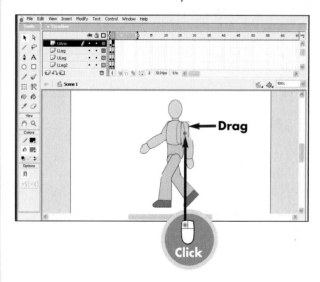

**Drag**  **Click**

## 15 Rotate and Move the Lower Arm

Now, use the **Free Transform** tool to rotate the lower arm slightly, and move it into position beneath the upper arm. If you are viewing the Stage in outline mode, you should see the outline of the first arm in the preceding frame.

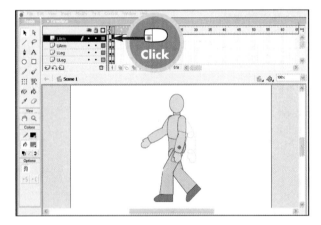

## 16 Move the Back Arm

Repeat the process for the back arm, moving it one-fifth the distance toward the opposite position. You will probably need to hide the torso layer while you do this. The example here shows the finished result while the torso is hidden.

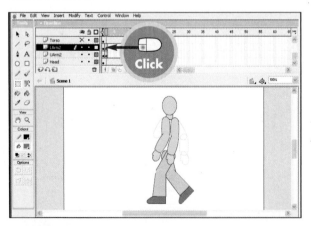

## 17 Move the Legs

Now, adjust the legs in a similar manner, showing and hiding layers as necessary to help keep track of which parts are being moved. When you are done, your character should be complete in the second frame.

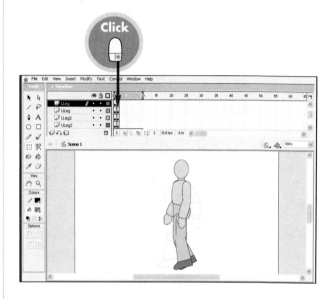

## 18 The Halfway Mark

Continue in this manner, adding keyframes in each layer and moving the body parts toward the halfway position in frame 5. The limbs should now be in the opposite position from the first frame, as shown here.

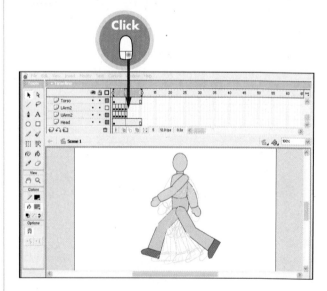

## 19 Return to the Original Position

Now that you've reached the halfway point, returning the limbs back to their original positions is much easier because you can use the outlines from the preceding steps as a guide to position the parts on their return.

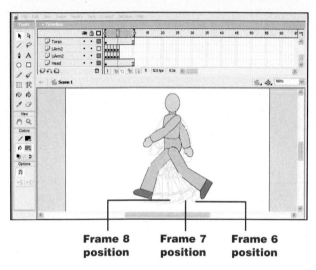

Frame 8 position    Frame 7 position    Frame 6 position

## 20 Use Copy and Paste

You can also use the clipboard to create the return frames. Select one of the layers from frame 4 and copy it into the clipboard. Add a blank keyframe (**Insert**, **Blank Keyframe**) in frame 6 of the same layer. Then choose **Edit**, **Paste in Place** to paste from the Clipboard into frame 6. Repeat to copy frame 3 into frame 7, and frame 2 into frame 8.

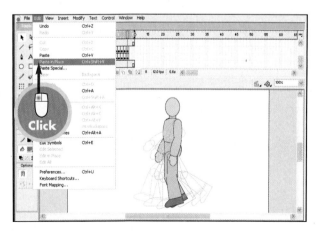

## 21 Delete the Extra Frames

If, at the end, you discover that you've created too many frames for your walk cycle (like we did here), all you need to do is delete the extra frames from the head and torso layers. Click in frame 9 of each layer and select **Insert**, **Remove Frames** twice. Now you should have eight frames total.

## 22 Save and Test

Save your movie (**File**, **Save**). To view the movie, select **Control**, **Loop Playback**, and then select **Control**, **Play**. The character's limbs should move smoothly as though he is walking across the Stage.

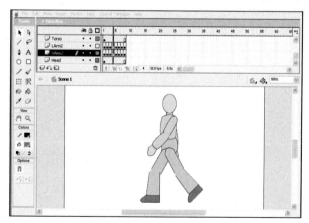

Task

# 5

# Adding Navigation and Interactivity

**W**ith buttons and actions in your Macromedia Flash movies, your visitor can navigate through your Web site as he or she chooses. A button is a clickable hot spot that typically has four states: Up, Over, Down, and Hit. You can design your buttons so that they appear differently in the Up, Over, and Down state, and use the Hit area to define the portion of the button that responds to the user interaction.

Button actions determine how a button functions in one or more of these states. For example, you can assign an action that opens another movie or Web page when the user clicks a button, or hover over a button to display a submenu of additional options. You'll learn how to create buttons of these types in the following tasks.

# How to Create a Basic Button

**A** *button* is a unique type of symbol that enables the user to navigate to other areas of your site or perform other interactive functions. Buttons consist of three visible frames that represent the appearance of the button (Up, Over, and Down). A fourth frame (Hit), which is invisible, defines the area that responds to the cursor. This task shows you how to create a basic button that uses all four button frames.

## ❶ Create a New Symbol

With nothing selected on the Stage, select **Insert, New Symbol**, or use the keyboard shortcut (⌘-**F8**) [**Ctrl+F8**]. The Create New Symbol dialog box appears.

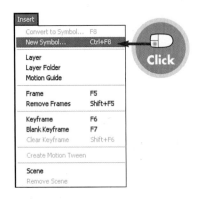

## ❷ Choose the Button Behavior

Enter a name for the new button (such as Home Button as shown here) in the **Name** field. From the **Behavior** section, select the **Button** radio button. Click **OK** to enter symbol-editing mode.

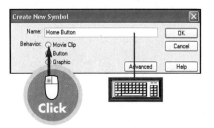

## ❸ Create the Up Frame

The first frame (Up) represents the appearance of the button before the user hovers over or clicks the button. It already contains a keyframe. Use the drawing tools, import a graphic, or drag a symbol from the library to create the Up frame. Your button can contain more than one layer if you desire.

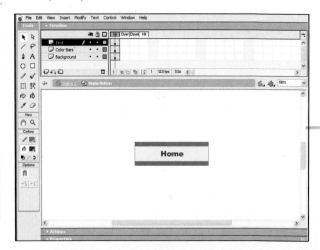

## ④ Create the Over Frame

The Over frame represents the button when the cursor hovers over it. Click in the Over frame, and then select **Insert, Keyframe** (or press **F6**) to create a keyframe. Put a new keyframe in the Over frame in each layer. Next, change the color of the button, text, or other areas so that the Over frame differs from the Up frame.

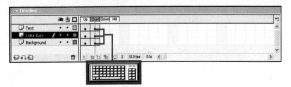

### How to Hint

## Creating Text-Only Buttons

When you create text-only buttons, keep in mind that if your Hit frame contains just the letters of the text, the button responds only when the cursor is directly over a letter. For the Hit frame of a text-only button, create a new layer and name it **Hit**. Add a keyframe in the Hit frame only, and create a solid rectangle that is large enough to cover the text completely. This rectangle will be invisible during runtime but creates a Hit area that is easier to use.

## ⑤ Create the Down Frame

Repeat step 4 for the Down frame, which represents the appearance of the button when it is pressed. Again, make changes to the appearance of the button to represent the Down state.

## ⑥ Create the Hit Frame

The Hit state defines the portion of the button that responds to the mouse. It should be equal to or larger than the button. It is "invisible" during runtime, so you need not be concerned with how it looks. Here, a keyframe is inserted in the Background layer to define the hit area.

# How to Create an Animated Button

**T**o create an animated button, you can insert a movie clip into the Up, Over, or Down frame. Most often, you'll see the movie clip in the Over state to respond when the user hovers over the mouse. Here's a basic task that shows you how to use movie clips to create an animated button that flashes an LED when the mouse hovers over the button. The same principles can be used for any other animated button.

## ❶ Set the Grid and Choose Colors

Turn on the grid (**View, Grid, Show Grid**) and the snap to grid feature (**View, Grid, Snap to Grid**) if desired. Select black for a stroke color and a red radial gradient for the fill color.

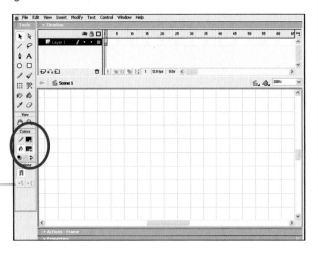

## ❷ Create the Static LED Symbol

Draw a circle that is two grid squares wide and two grid squares high. Select the outline and the fill, and select **Insert, Convert to Symbol** (⌘-**F8**) [**Ctrl+F8**]. Name the symbol **LED** and select **Movie Clip** for the behavior type. Click **OK** to create the symbol.

## ❸ Create the LED Movie Clip

With the instance of the LED selected on the Stage, select **Insert, Convert to Symbol** (**F8** for Windows or Mac). Enter **Animated LED** for the name, and again select **Movie Clip** for the behavior. Then click **OK** to create the symbol.

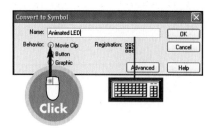

## ④ Add Keyframes to the Movie Clip

Double-click the LED movie clip on the Stage to enter symbol-editing mode. Insert keyframes (**F6**) at frames 6 and 10. This adds copies of the LED into all the frames.

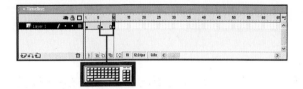

## ⑤ Add a Color Effect

To enhance the LED, click to select the keyframe in the sixth frame; then click the symbol on the Stage. From the **Properties** window, select **Tint** from the **Color** drop-down list. Select bright red for the color (RGB 255, 0, 0), and set the **Tint** value to **75%**.

## ⑥ Create the Tweens

Click the keyframe in the first frame, and select **Insert, Create Motion Tween**. Click the keyframe in the sixth frame, and select **Insert, Create Motion Tween** again. Exit symbol-editing mode and select **Control, Test Movie** to test the animation. You should see the LED blink.

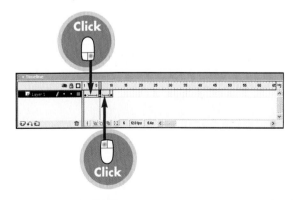

## ⑦ Build More Button Symbols

Use the **Insert, New Symbol** command to create the remaining symbols for your button, such as a background on which to place the LED, and the text that labels the button. Add these symbols to your library.

## ⑧ Put the Button Together

Create a new movie (**File, New**); then select **Insert, New Symbol**. Name the new symbol **Home Button**, and select **Button** as the behavior. Click **OK** to enter symbol-editing mode.

## ⑨ Add the Button Symbols to the Up State

Open the library that contains the symbols you created in steps 1–7. Place the button background, text, and static LED (here, called LED) on separate layers in the Up frame.

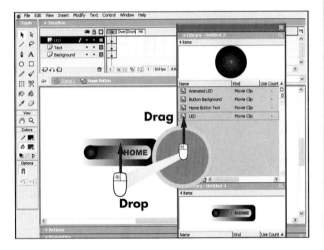

## ⑩ Create the Over and Down States

Insert keyframes (**F6**) on each layer of the Over state and Down state.

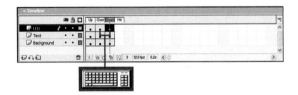

## ⑪ Add the Animated LED to the Over State

Click to select the Over frame in the LED layer, and delete the static LED. Then, drag the animated LED to the same location.

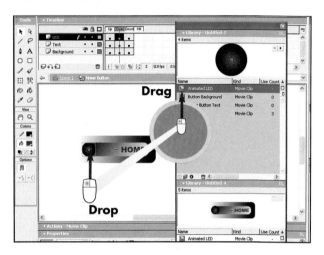

## ⑫ Create the Hit Frame

Add a keyframe (**F6**) in the Background layer of the Hit frame to create the Hit area. The button is now complete.

## 13 Add the Button to the Stage

Drag the Home Button symbol from your movie library to the Stage. Create additional buttons as required, changing the text as necessary.

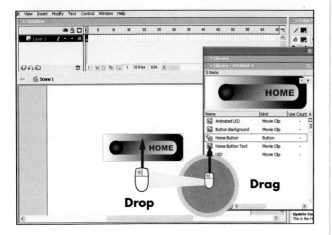

**Drop**

**Drag**

## Testing the Animated Button

Because the button contains a movie clip, you need to select the **Control, Test Movie** command to test the button animation.

## The Animated Frame

You can get very creative with the animated frame in the button: wave a flag, pop out a menu, display fireworks, or create just about any other animation you want. Remember, though, not to make the animation so large that the user has to wait for it to download. Keep it small and trim.

# How to Assign Actions to Buttons

If you click the buttons you created in the previous tasks, you'll probably notice that they don't *do* anything yet. Buttons won't work unless you assign one or more actions to them. The most common uses for buttons are to navigate to another portion of your site or play another movie. You can also create buttons that start or stop the current movie, turn off sounds, or submit a form for processing. You assign actions with the Actions panel, which is described in the following steps.

## 1 Select the Button

Design all your buttons and place them on the Stage. Click with the Arrow tool to select the button to which you want to assign an action. The **Properties** window displays the default option of **Track As Button** in the **Options for Buttons** drop-down list.

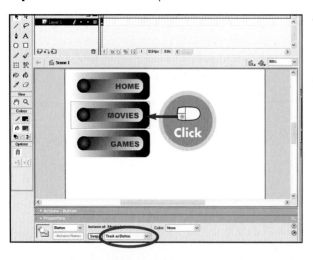

## 2 Open the Button Actions Panel

Select **Window, Actions** or press **F2** to display the Actions panel beneath the Stage. The header of the panel should read **Actions-Button**.

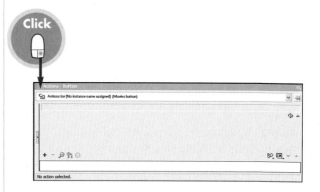

## 3 Open the Actions List

Click the plus sign (**+**) in the lower-left corner of the Actions panel. Select **Actions** from the menu to display a submenu of action commands from which to choose. This chapter discusses some of the options you will find in the Movie Control and Browser/Network submenus.

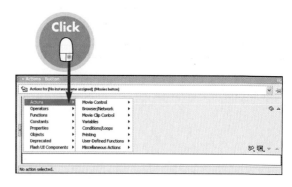

## 4 Permanently Display the Actions List

To display the Actions list in a pane at the left side of the Actions panel, click the small arrow at the left side of the Actions panel. In this mode, you can double-click or drag an action to add it to the script window. Click the arrow again to hide the Actions list pane.

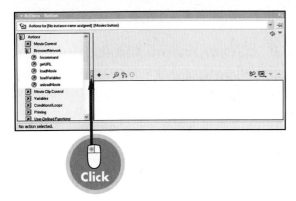

## 5 Assign the Action

To create a button that opens a Web page, select **Actions**, **Browser/Network**, **getURL**. The Button Actions panel displays several variables for you to complete. The Get URL command requires that you enter a URL. You can optionally select the window type in which the Web page appears (self, blank, parent, or top) and whether to send variables when the button is pressed.

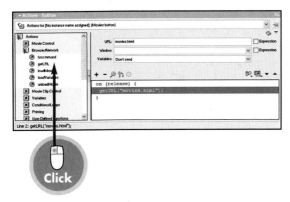

## 6 Edit the ActionScript

The ActionScript code appears beneath the options list. Highlight a line of code to display the associated options that are available for that line. For example, when you highlight the first line of code, you can edit the button so that you can go to a URL when you release the mouse button or when you press the "U" key.

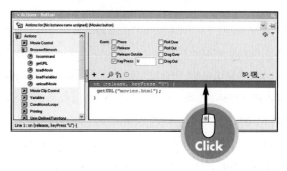

# How to Use Go to and Play Buttons

**G**o to and Play buttons are commonly used to jump to another frame or scene in a movie and to play the movie from that point. The following steps guide you through the process of creating a Go to and Play button.

## ❶ Choose the Action

Select the button on the Stage to which you want to assign the action, and open the **Button Actions** window, as described in the previous task. From the **Movie Control** section, select **goto**.

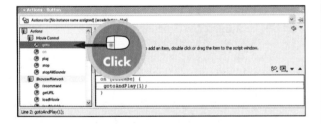

## ❷ Go to Another Frame

By default, a Go to and Play button navigates to the first frame in the current scene of your movie. To go to any other frame in the current movie, simply enter a new frame number in the **Frame** field, as shown here.

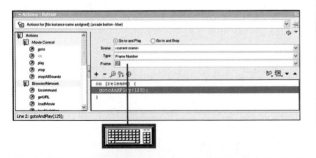

## ❸ Other Frame Choices

From the **Type** drop-down list, select **Frame Label** to jump to a specific frame to which you have assigned a label, or select **Next Frame** to advance to the next frame in the current scene. You can also select **Previous Frame** to return to the previous frame in the current scene. Select **Expression** and then enter the expression in the frame field to select a frame number by an expression that produces a value (such as **currentframe + 10**).

## ④ Go to Another Scene

To jump to another scene in the same movie, select an option from the **Scene** drop-down list. Select **<next scene>** to go to the next scene, as listed in the Scene panel **Shift+F2** opens the Scene panel). Select **<previous scene>** to go to the scene immediately before the current scene. The drop-down list also enables you to select any scene in the current movie by name.

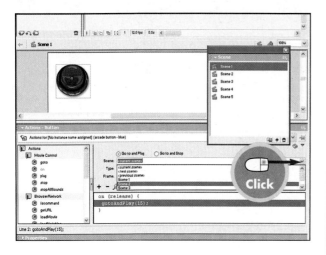

## ⑤ Go to a Frame in Another Scene

You can also combine the Scene and Frame options to jump to a specific frame in another scene. Simply select the scene from the **Scene** drop-down list and then select the frame number as outlined in steps 2 and 3.

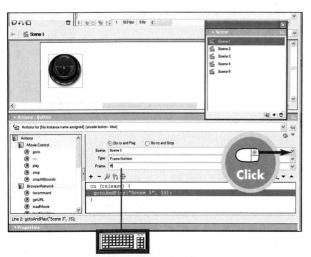

## ⑥ Change the Button Action

By default, the Go to and Play action takes place when the user releases the mouse button. To change this, highlight the line of code that reads **on (release)**. Select from the available options shown in this figure. Of particular interest is the Key Press option, which allows you to enter a hot key that performs the action.

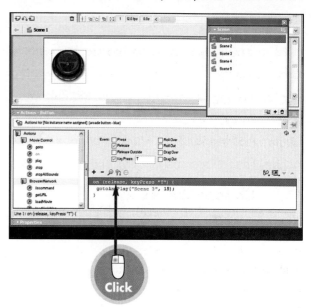

### How to Hint

## More Sophistication

Flash also allows you to create Go to and Stop buttons, which go to a frame or scene in a movie and stop at the designated frame. For an example of how you can use Go to and Stop buttons, refer to Project 2, "Constructing a Hierarchical Menu." This project shows you how to build the menu step by step and how to assign the actions to the buttons.

# How to Create a Rollover Menu

The following task shows you how to create a rollover menu. During the process, you'll learn a little bit more about how the Go to and Play command works. You'll also learn how to create a button that responds to more than one mouse action. The rollover menu fades in a picture when you hover the mouse over a button and then fades out the picture again when you move the mouse away from the button.

## ❶ Add the Content

Add the content that you want to display through the rollover menu onto the Stage. Here, seven JPG images are converted to Flash symbols and placed on seven different layers.

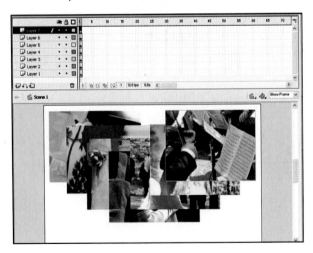

## ❷ Stagger the Images

The first item will fade in and out between frames 1 and 20, the second from frame 21 to 40, and so on. Drag the frame 1 keyframe for Layer 2 and up to the appropriate starting number (Layer 2 to frame 21, Layer 3 to frame 41, Layer 4 to frame 61, and so on).

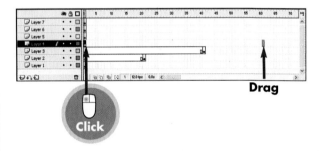

## ❸ Add Keyframes for the Tween

Return to the first frame for Layer 1. Add keyframes (**F6**) at frames 10 (for the fade in) and 20 (for the fade out).

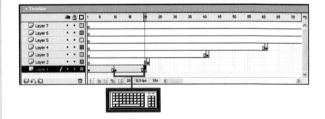

## ④ Add the Fades

To make the object invisible on the first frame (1) and the last frame (20), display the **Properties** window (**Ctrl+F3**), and then click the item on the Stage. Select **Alpha** from the **Color** drop-down list; then set the **Alpha** to **0%** using the slider or the text box. The middle keyframe (at frame 10 for the first object) remains opaque.

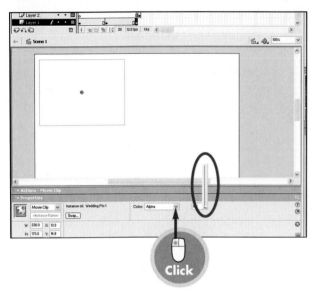

Click

## ⑤ Create the Tweens

Click the first keyframe at Frame 1, and select **Insert, Create Motion Tween**. Click the second keyframe at frame 10, and repeat the command. When you drag the Timeline indicator over the first 20 frames, you should see the object fade in and out.

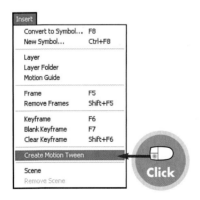

Click

## ⑥ Complete All Tweens

Repeat steps 4 and 5 for the remaining objects, creating a fade-in during the first 10 frames and a fade-out during the last 10 frames of its place on the Timeline. Seven sets of tweens in this example consume 140 frames total.

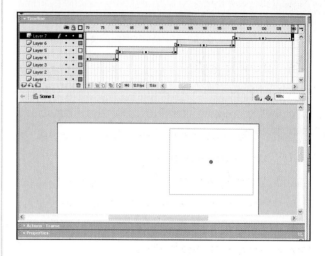

## ⑦ Add Actions Layer

Create a new layer and label it **Actions**. Frame 1 automatically contains a keyframe. Add additional keyframes (**F6**) at the end of each fade-in (frames 10, 30, 50, and so on) and at the end of each fade-out (frames 20, 40, 60, and so on).

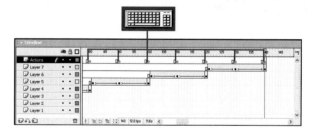

## (8) Add Stop Actions

Now you need to add a stop action to each keyframe in the Actions layer (except the first). Click the keyframe in frame 10 and open the **Actions** panel (**F9**). From the **Movie Control** actions list, double-click **stop**. Repeat this for keyframes starting at frame 20 until you reach the end.

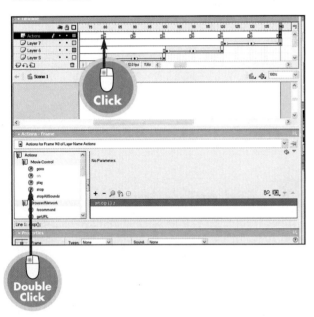

## (9) Edit Multiple Frames

To aid in positioning the buttons, click the **Edit Multiple Frames** button and select **Onion All** from the **Onion Markers** menu. This displays all the objects and shows you where there is free space remaining for button placement.

## (10) Add the Buttons

Create a new Button layer, and drag one button for each image from the library onto the Stage. (Select **Window**, **Common Libraries Buttons**, **Oval Library** to select the button shown here.) Label the buttons appropriately for each of the objects that you created in steps 1–8.

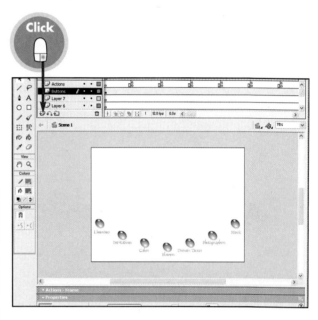

## (11) Assign Roll Over for the Fade-In Action

Click the first button. To fade the object in when the user rolls over the mouse, double-click **goto**. Keep the default of Go to and Play. Enter **1** for the frame number. Next, highlight the code line that reads **on (release)**. Uncheck **Release**, and check **Roll Over**.

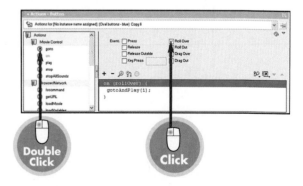

## 12 Assign Roll Out for the Fade-Out Action

Select the last line of ActionScript code. To fade out the object when the user rolls out from the button, double-click **goto** from the **Movie Control** actions list. Keep the default of Go to and Play, and enter **11** for the frame number. Next, highlight the code line that reads **on** (`release`). Uncheck **Release**, and check **Roll Out**.

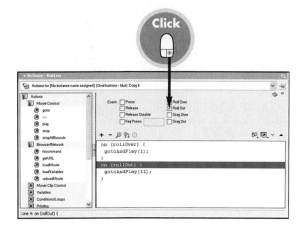

## 13 Complete the Buttons

Finally, define what the button does when the user clicks it, highlight the last line of ActionScript code. Select the desired action from the **Actions** list. (Here, the **Goto** action plays a different scene when the user releases the mouse button.) The first button is now complete.

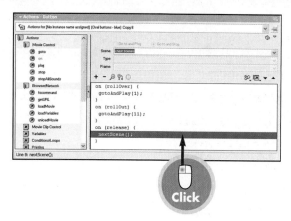

## Completing the Project

After you've completed the first button, you need to repeat steps 11–13 for the remaining buttons. You can copy the code from the first button and paste it into the code area for the other buttons. For the second button, use frame 21 for the fade in (rollover) and frame 31 for the fade out (rollout). For the third button, use frames 41 and 51, and so on for each successive button.

# How to Test Buttons and Menus

**A**fter you define the various states of the button, you should test to ensure that the button states work as intended. Normally, you should disable buttons while you are working on your animation so you can select them, move them, and so on. Enable your buttons when you want the buttons to react to your mouse movements as they would in the final animation. This task shows how to ensure the visible behavior of the button works according to your design.

## ❶ Select the Button

A button acts like any other symbol or instance on the Stage until you enable it. To select a button, click it with the Arrow tool or drag a selection box around the button to select it.

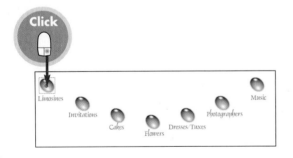

## ❷ Enable the Button

To ensure that the button responds to mouse clicks, select **Control, Enable Simple Buttons**. A check mark appears next to this option when button actions are enabled. Alternatively, use the keyboard shortcut (⌘-**Opt-B**) [**Ctrl+Alt+B**].

## ❸ Hover Over and Click the Button

Hover the mouse over the button to verify that it changes to the Hover state. Click the button to verify that it changes to the Down state.

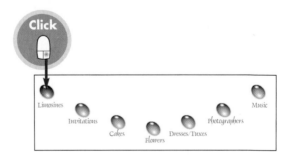

## 4 Test Other Actions

To test other actions, such as the RollOver and RollOut states that are used in the Rollover menu, use the Test Movie command. Select **Control, Test Movie** to open the movie in a test window.

## 5 Roll Over the Button

Roll over the button to verify that it responds to the mouse action. Then, move the mouse away from the button to verify that the button responds as designed.

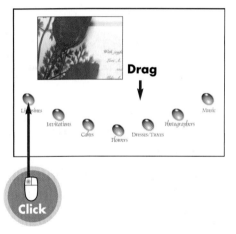

## 6 Exit the Test Screen

To exit the test screen, click the small **X** in the upper-right corner of the test window.

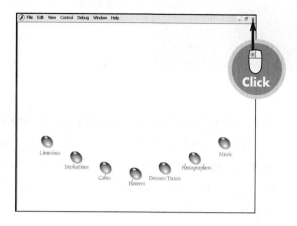

How to Hint

# Constructing a Hierarchical Menu

**H**ierarchical menus are real space savers because you don't have to display all the menu choices in a lengthy list. They also present your navigational structure in a clear, easy-to-understand format, similar to how they are used in most software programs. In this task, you learn how to create a hierarchical menu in Flash.

## 1 Create the Movie and the First Layer

Create a new movie using the shortcut (⌘-**N**) [**Ctrl+N**]. Double-click the **Layer 1** name in the Timeline and rename it **MenuLev1** (short for Menu Level 1).

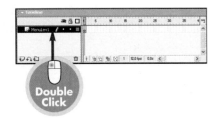

## 2 Add Two More Layers

Click the **Insert Layer** button to add a new layer. Double-click the second layer name and change it to **MenuLev2** (short for Menu Level 2). Finally, insert a third layer, and name this layer **Actions**.

## 3 Label the First Actions Layer Frame

Click the first frame in the Actions layer. In the **Properties** panel (⌘-**F3**) [**Ctrl+F3**] and enter **Start** for the frame label.

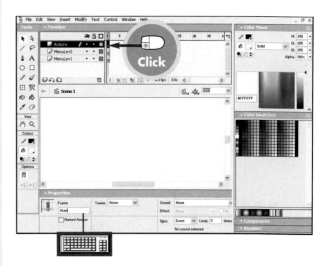

## 4 Add Keyframes for Each Main Menu Choice

Determine the number of top-level menu choices you want to create. For each, you need to insert a keyframe (**F6**) in the Actions layer. Add a keyframe on frame 11 for the first choice, on frame 21 for the second choice, and so on. Here, keyframes are added for three main menu choices, at frames 11, 21, and 31.

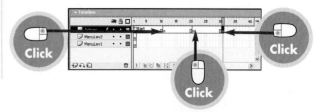

## ⑤ Add the Frame Actions

The first frame of each section should contain a Stop action that prevents the movie from playing through to the end. Select the keyframe on frame 1, and open the **Actions** panel (**F9**). From the **Movie Control** section (under the Actions section), double-click the stop action. Repeat this for each of the remaining keyframes (at frames 11, 21, 31, and so on).

## ⑥ Add the Final Frames

To increase the length of the final menu choice to 10 frames (the same length as the others), insert a frame (**F5**) in the **Actions** layer in the 10th frame of the last segment. In the example shown, the frame is added at frame 40.

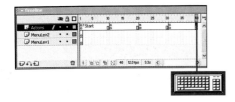

## ⑦ Label the Menu Sections

To assign a label to each of the menu sections, return to the **Properties** panel (⌘-**F3**) [**Ctrl+F3**]. Select the keyframe on frame 11. Then enter a name that is descriptive of the menu choice you want to display (such as **Music** shown here), and press **Enter** to assign the label.

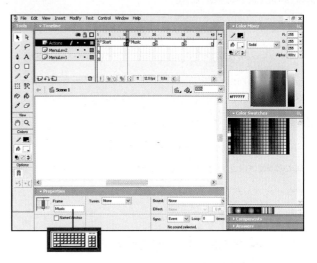

## ⑧ Label the Menu Sections

In a similar manner, repeat step 7 to assign the labels to the additional sections (such as **Films** on frame 21, **Books** on frame 31, and so on for each additional menu choice you created).

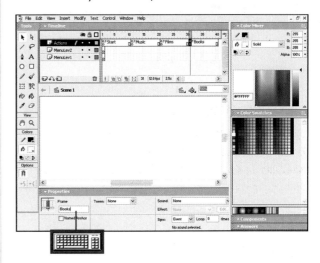

## ⑨ Create the Main Menu Background

Add or create a background symbol on which to place the buttons for the main menu. Add the symbol to the first frame of the MenuLev1 layer. Here, three rounded rectangles with dotted outlines are grouped together and converted to a symbol.

## ⑩ Create the Main Menu Buttons

Create the buttons for your main menu, and add them to the first frame of the MenuLev1 layer. Three menu choices (Music, Films, and Books) are created for this example.

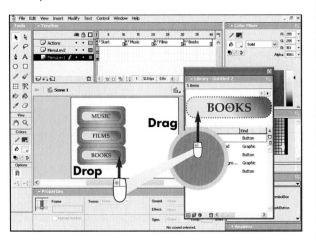

Drag

Drop

## ⑪ Display the Main Menu Buttons in All Frames

The main menu buttons should appear on the Stage throughout all the frames in the movie. To accomplish this, add a frame (**F5**) in frame 40 of the MenuLev1 layer.

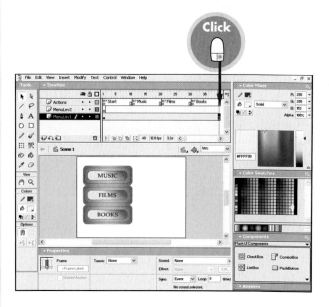

Click

## ⑫ Create a Keyframe for the Menu1 Submenu

Select **MenuLev2** as the current layer, and add a keyframe (**F6**) on frame 11 (the start of the Menu1 section). Frames 11–20 in the MenuLev2 layer will be used to display the submenu for menu choice #1.

## 13 Add the Submenu Background

Add or create a background symbol on which to place the sublevel button sets (you'll need one submenu set for each top-level menu). Here, two rounded rectangles and some dots are converted to a symbol. The dots help identify which menu item is selected by the user. Add the first submenu background to frame 11 on the MenuLev2 layer.

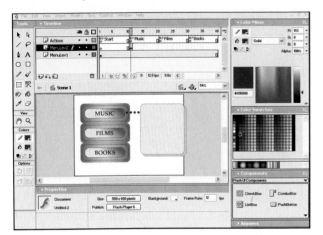

## 14 Create and Add Submenu 1 Buttons

Create the buttons for the submenus that appears when Menu1, 2, or 3 is selected, and add them to your library. Drag the Menu1 buttons to frame 11 on layer MenuLev2, and position them on the background. Five submenu choices are created for this example. Use the **Align** panel (⌘-K) [**Ctrl+K**] to align and space the buttons evenly.

**Drag buttons from library**

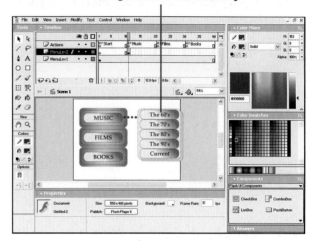

## 15 Create and Add Submenu 2 Buttons

Add a keyframe on frame 21 of the MenuLev2 layer. Reposition the button background so that it aligns with the next main menu item. (**Control-Click**) [**right-click**] the first submenu button and select **Swap Symbol**. Replace it with the appropriate button for menu 2.

## 16 Complete Remaining Submenus

Repeat the same steps on frame 31 for the third set of submenu buttons, and frames 41, 51, and so on. Swap the Submenu2 buttons with the buttons that appear on the menu level you are working on.

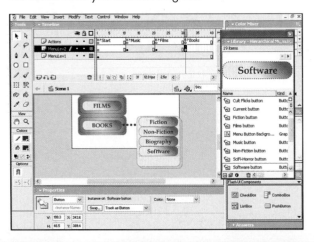

## 17 Complete the Layer

Complete the layer by adding a frame (**F5**) in frame 40 (or whichever frame number you have as the last frame in the Actions layer).

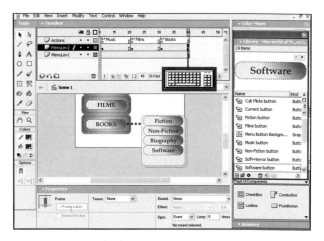

## 18 Assign the On Release Action to Main Menu Buttons

When the user presses a menu button, the movie advances to the frame that displays the appropriate submenu. To accomplish this, **Control-click** (Mac) or **right-click** (Windows) a menu button and select **Actions** from the submenu. From the **Movie Control** actions, double-click **on**. By default, the Release event is selected. Uncheck **Release**, and check **Roll Over**.

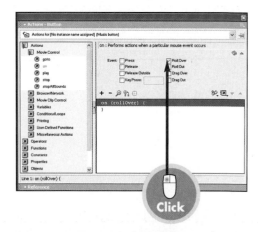

### 19 Assign Actions to the Main Menu Buttons

Position the cursor on the last line of ActionScript code (the bracket). Then, double-click **goto** from the **Movie Control** actions list. Select the **Go to and Stop** radio button, and enter the appropriate frame number (such as `Frame 11` for the Music menu) in the **Frame** field. Repeat these steps for the other main menu buttons, assigning them to the appropriate frame in your movie.

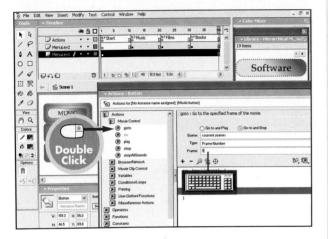

### 20 Assign Actions to the Submenu Buttons

Your submenu buttons can open other Flash movies, navigate to Web pages on your site, or play multimedia files. In the example shown, the 60s button opens a Web page called `60smovies.html`. The getURL action in the Browser/Network category allows you to link to a URL.

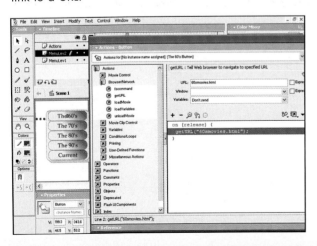

### 21 Save the Project

After you assign all the actions to your submenu buttons, select **File, Save** or use the keyboard shortcut (⌘-S) [Ctrl+S] to save your movie project.

### 22 Test the Movie

Select **Control, Test Movie** to test your submenu. When you hover over a main menu item, the appropriate submenu should appear. When you click a submenu button, you should jump to a Web page, open another movie, or perform any other action that you assigned to the submenu button.

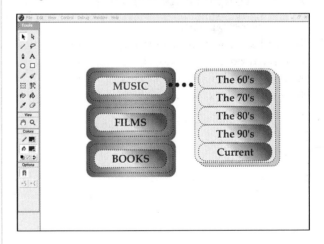

Task

**6**

# Sounds

You can create a richer multimedia experience for your visitors by adding sound to your Macromedia Flash projects. For example, you'll often hear sounds that respond to mouse movements when the user clicks or hovers over a button. In addition, you can seamlessly blend dialog, music, and sound effects to create a soundtrack that enhances the visual portion of your project. Flash provides some basic tools that allow you to import sounds to your movies and manipulate the volumes. You can add one or more sounds to your project and layer them to create interesting music soundtracks for your projects. This section shows you how.

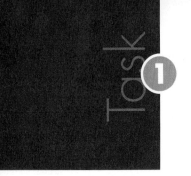

# How to Import Sounds and Add Them to a Movie

To use sound in your animation, you must first import the sound into your Macromedia Flash Library. Then, you add it to the movie. It's always a good idea to keep the sounds you add to your animation on a separate layer. In fact, you might consider making a new layer for each sound you add. Flash treats each sound layer as a separate track of audio and mixes all sounds together in the final movie.

## 1 Select File, Import

To import one or more sounds, select **File**, **Import**, or use the keyboard shortcut (⌘-**R**) [**Ctrl+R**].

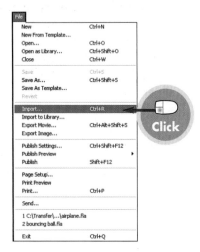

## 2 Select the File

In the **Import** dialog box (Windows) or Mac file chooser, navigate to the folder that contains the WAV (PC), AIFF (Mac), or MP3 (either platform) file on your system. After you select the file(s), select (**Import**) [**Open**]. The files are added to the Flash project and appear in the Library just as any other imported media does.

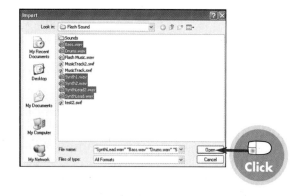

## How to Hint

### Sounds from the Common Library

If you need sounds for button clicks or mouse moves, Flash provides a library of sounds you can use freely. To find them, select **Window**, **Common Libraries**, **Sounds**.

## ③ Create a Sound Layer

To create the sound layer, click the **Insert Layer** button at the lower-left corner of the Timeline. Alternatively, (Ctrl-click) [right-click] an existing layer, and then select **Insert Layer** from the menu. The new layer appears directly above the currently selected layer. To label the layer with a descriptive name, double-click the current layer name and type the new name.

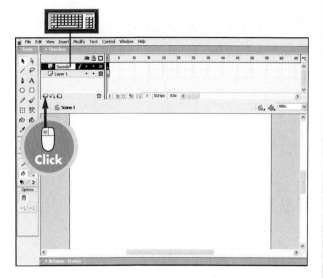

## ④ Add a Keyframe

If you want to start the sound in a frame other than the first frame, use the keyboard shortcut **F6** to add a keyframe to the desired frame. Then click to select the target keyframe. Select **Window**, **Properties** to open the Properties window.

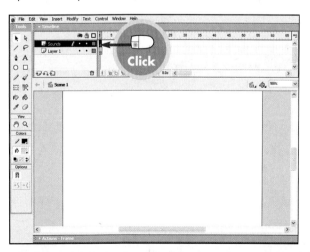

## ⑤ Insert the Sound

From the **Sound** drop-down list in the Properties window, select the name of the sound you want to insert at the selected keyframe. This adds the sound to your project at the selected keyframe.

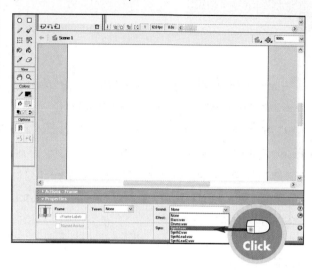

## ⑥ Drag a Sound to the Stage

You can also drag a sound from your movie library onto the Stage. After you select a target keyframe as in step 4, select **Window**, **Library** to open the Library window. Click the name of the sound in the list. Now, click and drag either the waveform of the sound or the name of the sound onto the Stage.

# How to Choose a Synchronization Option

After you've added the sound to your movie, you must choose how the sound behaves in relation to the rest of the movie. You can specify the behavior of the sound symbol (which affects all instances of the sound) or individual instances. In either case, use the Sync drop-down list to set the desired option.

## 1 Select the Sound

To edit the sound symbol, select the desired sound from your current movie library, or click the sound in the Timeline.

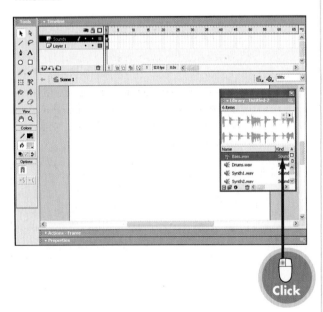

## 2 Choose a Sync Option

Open the **Properties** window, and select an option from the **Sync** drop-down list.

## Keeping Up with Synchronized Sounds

When you stream sound over the Internet, Flash attempts to play the sound normally as it delivers the sound to the user. If your movie is complex, Flash might reduce visual quality or drop visual frames to keep pace with the streaming sound.

## Think of the Possibilities

Subtle sounds can shape the overall experience in ways that the audience can't consciously identify. Don't underestimate the importance of music, dialog, and sound effects. Because audio causes your final file size to increase rapidly, put careful thought into where and how to use audio in your movies.

## 3 Use Event Sync

Select **Event** from the **Sync** drop-down list in the Sound panel to play a sound to completion—even if the movie stops or ends, or if you start another instance of the same sound while the first plays (as shown here).

**Sound 1 starts**  **Sound 2 starts**  **Sound 1 ends**  **Sound 2 ends**

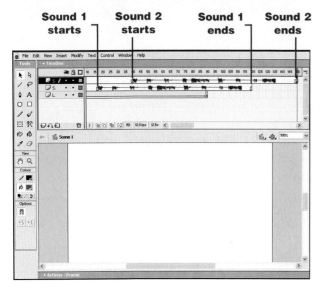

## 4 Use Start Sync

Select **Start** to prevent "layering" of multiple instances of the same sound. If you add a second instance of the same sound, it begins to play after the first instance ends.

**First instance starts**  **First instance ends, second starts**

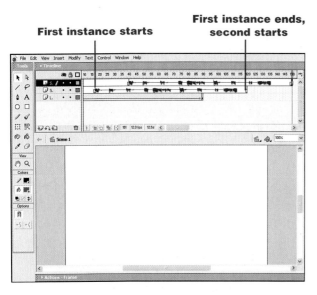

## 5 Use Stop Sync

The Stop sync option ends a selected sound at a specific keyframe. Press **F6** to add a keyframe where you want the sound to end. Select a sound from the Timeline or from the **Sound** drop-down list, and then select **Stop** from the **Sync** drop-down list. The sound ends at the keyframe location even if the length of the sound extends beyond it.

**Sound stops**

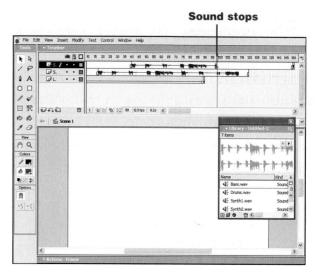

## 6 Use Stream Sync

Use the **Stream** sync option to stream sounds for delivery over the Internet. When you stream a sound, Flash forces the animation to keep pace with the sound, even if it has to drop frames to do it. A streamed sound plays until the movie stops. Here, a streamed sound is shown in the bandwidth profiler.

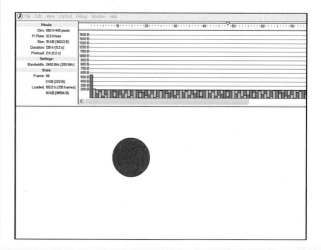

# How to Add Sound to a Button

**B**uttons seem more real when you add clicks or other sound effects that occur when users click or hover over them. When you add sounds to a master button symbol, the sounds will be present in every instance of the symbol that you place on the Stage. If you edit a master button symbol in a shared symbol library, the sound extends to any movie that includes a button that is linked back to that master symbol.

## ① Open the Library

Select **Window**, **Library** to open the movie library (or **File**, **Open As Library** to open a shared movie library). If you don't have a button of your own, select **Window**, **Common Libraries**, **Buttons** and drag and drop the button onto the Stage to add it to your current movie library.

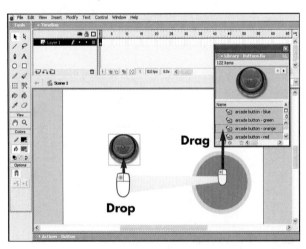

## ② Select the Button

From your movie library (**Window**, **Library**), (Ctrl-click) [right-click] the button name you want to modify. Then select **Edit** from the pop-up menu to enter symbol-editing mode. Alternatively, you can double-click the button symbol.

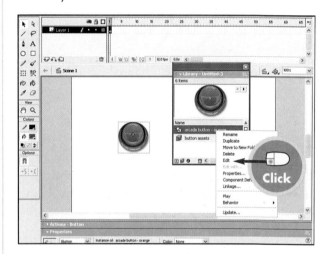

## ③ Insert a Sound Layer

Select the topmost layer in the button Timeline, and click the **Insert Layer** button to create a new layer above it. Name the new layer **Sounds**.

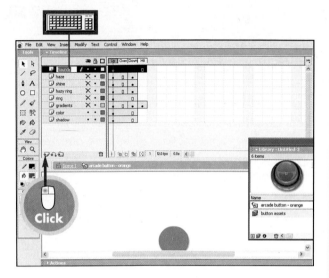

## ④ Add Keyframes

As you learned in Part 5, "Adding Navigation and Interactivity," a button has three main states: Up, Over, and Down. To assign a sound to any or each of these states, click in the frame that corresponds to the desired state (the Down state is most common). Then press **F6** to add a keyframe on the sound layer.

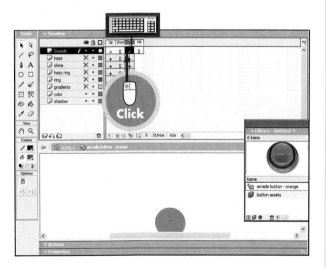

## ⑤ Add the Sound

Use one of the methods you learned in Task 3, "How to Add Sound to a Button," to add the desired sound to the new keyframe. After you add your sound, click the **Page** tab (Mac) or **Scene** tab (Windows) to exit symbol-editing mode.

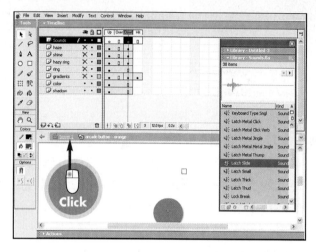

How to Hint

## Testing the Button Sound

There are two ways to test your button sounds after you place them on the Stage. The easiest way is to select **Control**, **Enable Simple Buttons**; then you click the button to hear the sound play. Select the command again to return the buttons to an editable state. You can also select **Control**, **Test Movie** and click the button.

# How to Use Sound Effects

After you add a sound file to your movie, Flash allows you to perform basic editing functions on it, such as fading a sound in or out, changing volume, or editing the start and stop points. Effects are more noticeable if you add them to longer files, such as musical backgrounds.

## 1 Select the Sound

Click in the movie Timeline to select the sound you want to edit.

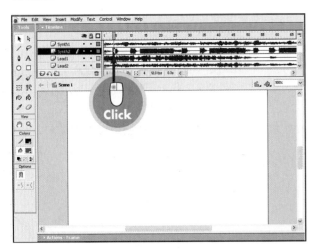

## 2 Open the Properties Window

If the Properties window is not open, select **Window**, **Properties**, or use the shortcut (⌘-**F3**) [**Ctrl+F3**].

## 3 Select the Effect

From the **Effect** drop-down menu, select the effect you want to apply to the sound. Options are discussed in the following steps. To view the results of the effects as shown here, click the **Edit** button at the right of the Effect drop-down list to display the Edit Envelope dialog box. The Effect drop-down list also appears in this dialog box.

## 4 Use the Left Channel or Right Channel

Select the **Left Channel** option to force the sound to play on the left side of the stereo spectrum (left or right). The volume of the left channel remains at maximum, and the right channel is turned off. The Right Channel option works similarly.

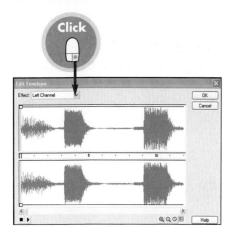

## 5 Use Directional Fades

Directional fades can enhance your movie when an object moves from left to right, or right to left. Select **Fade Left to Right** to start the sound in the left speaker. As the sound continues to play, it gradually shifts so that at the halfway point it plays through both speakers, and toward the end it plays in the right speaker. The Fade Right to Left option does the opposite.

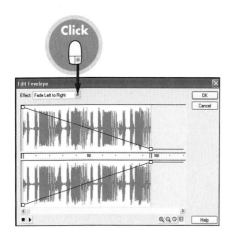

## 6 Fade In or Out

Your audience will appreciate that you fade music in rather than present them with a sudden blast of full-volume music. For musical backgrounds (especially loud ones), select **Fade In** to gradually fade the music in until it reaches full volume. The Fade Out option does the opposite—it gradually fades the sound from full volume to no volume over time.

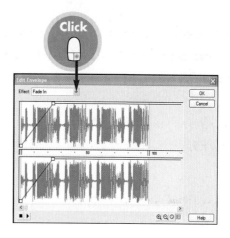

## 7 Customize Effects

Flash also allows you to create custom effects. If you have not already done so, click the **Edit** button that appears at the right of the Effect drop-down list. The Edit Envelope dialog box appears.

## **8** Choose Custom Effect

The sound wave for the left channel appears at the top of the dialog box, and the right channel appears at the bottom. The Effect drop-down list enables you to select any of the effect options discussed in steps 4–6. To create a custom effect, select **Custom** from the drop-down list.

## **9** Adjust Channel Volume

A single node appears at the beginning of the sound. Drag the node up to increase the volume of the sound, or drag it down to decrease the volume of the sound. To increase or decrease volume over time, click the volume line to add another node and drag it left or right to adjust the length of the volume adjustment.

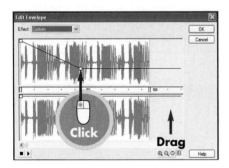

## **10** Adjust the Other Channel

When you add a node in one channel, a second node automatically appears at the same time location in the opposite channel. Simply drag the second node upward or downward to adjust the volume in the second channel.

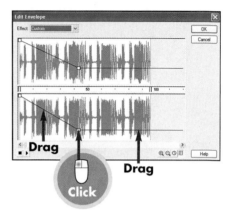

## **11** Add Additional Nodes

Repeat steps 9 and 10 to add more nodes that adjust the volume of the sound.

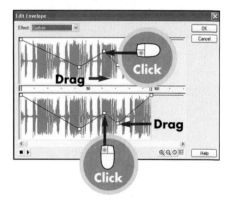

## ⑫ Review Your Effect

Click the **Play** button to preview the results of your effect. After you complete your custom effect, click **OK** to exit the Edit Envelope dialog box.

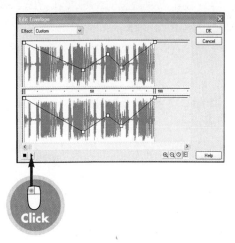

## ⑬ Create a Pan

To simulate a more complex pan, simply perform opposite volume effects in the left and right channels. Where you increase the volume in one channel, decrease the volume by the same amount in the other channel. This is how the Fade Left to Right and Fade Right to Left effects are accomplished.

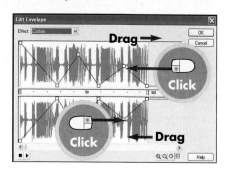

## Editing Looped Sounds

You can also create custom effects for looped sounds. This is explained in more detail in Task 5, "How to Loop Sounds."

# How to Loop Sounds

Flash enables you to loop sounds so that you can play them longer. This is ideal for creating soundtracks—instead of using a 1-minute audio file in the background while your movie plays, you can economize by using a smaller 6-second file (for example) and loop it 10 times. Now your project file is smaller and quicker to download. It's relatively easy to loop sounds, and you can add effects to the looped file.

## ❶ Find a Suitable Sound

Looped files sound best when you use a file that was specifically designed to loop—that is, a sound that plays seamlessly when repeated over and over. If you can easily determine where the sound ends or begins when it loops, you might want to select another one. Loops of 8–32 beats of music are usually sufficient enough for repetition, depending on the content.

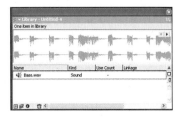

## ❷ Import the Sounds to Your Library

Select **File**, **Import** (or **File**, **Import to Library**), and locate the sound you want to add to your project. Select the file and click **Open** to place the file in your library.

## 3 Create a Sound Layer and Add a Keyframe

Create a sound layer in the Timeline, and press **F5** in the last frame in which you want the sound to play. For example, if your sound is 10 seconds long and your movie plays at 12 frames per second, you need 120 frames to play it once. If you want to loop it three times, you need at least 360 frames. Click in frame 360 and press **F5**.

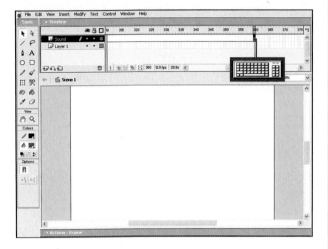

## 4 Add the Sound

Click the keyframe where you want the sound to start (or the first keyframe if you have not yet added any), and drag the sound from the library onto the Stage. The sound waveform appears in the Timeline.

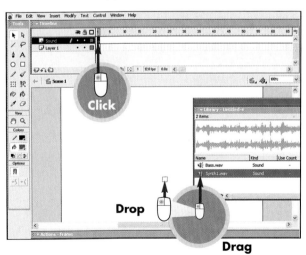

## 5 Specify Loop Quantity and Sync Options

Open the Properties window (**Window**, **Properties**) if it is not open. Click anywhere in the sound layer in the Timeline to display the sound options. In the **Loop** field, enter the number of times you want the sound to loop. Then, select your synchronization option as described in Task 2, "How to Choose a Synchronization Option."

## 6 Play the Sound

To play the sound in the movie, select **Control**, **Play** or press (**Return**) [**Enter**]. Depending on your sync option, the sound plays until the end of the last loop or until the last keyframe in the sound layer.

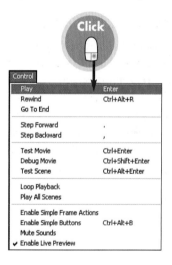

## 7 Add an Effect

To add effects to a looped sound, highlight the sound in the Timeline and click the **Edit** button in the Properties window. The Edit Envelope dialog box appears.

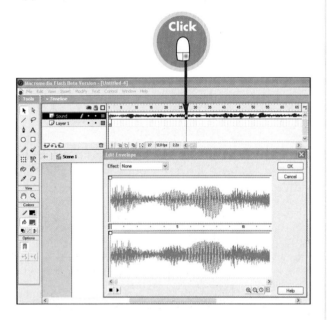

## 8 Zoom In or Out

If you want to view a larger portion of the waveform in the Edit Envelope window, use the **Zoom Out** magnifier until you see a larger segment. Use the **Zoom In** magnifier to move back in.

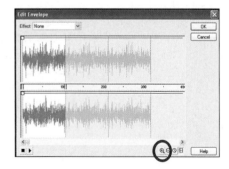

## 9 Choose an Effect

Select the desired effect from the **Effect** drop-down list. More than likely, you'll need to use a custom effect for your looped audio. For example, you might want to create a fade-in at the beginning and a fade-out at the end. Simply click the volume line to add nodes, and drag the nodes to increase or decrease the volume appropriately.

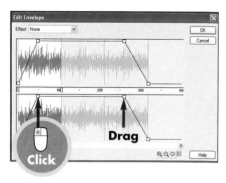

## 10 Start a Silent Segment

Suppose you want to silence the loops for a while but still keep things in the correct tempo (you'll need this knowledge for the next task). First, go to the location where you want the silence to start. Add two nodes at the same location, positioning the first one at maximum volume and the second at zero volume. This starts the break.

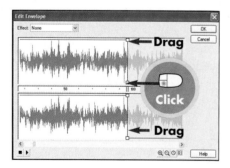

## 11 End a Silent Segment

Now, go to the location where you want the silence to end. Again, add two nodes at the same location. Position the first node at zero volume and the second at maximum volume. This ends the break.

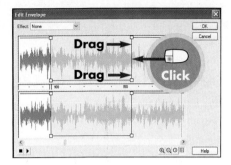

## 12 Preview the Sound

To preview the effect in the Edit Envelope dialog box, click the **Play** button in the lower-left corner. Continue making adjustments to the sound until you get the effect you desire.

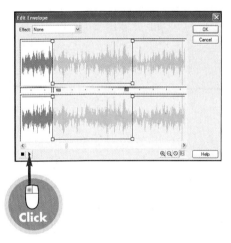

## 13 Return to the Main Timeline

Click **OK** to return to the Stage and the main Timeline. The looped waveform will not appear any different in the main Timeline window, but the effect is applied to the file. Press (**Return**) [**Enter**] to check it out.

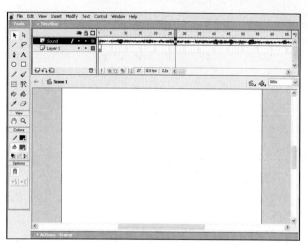

### How to Hint

## Viewing Loops in the Edit Envelope Dialog Box

When you look at a looped sound in the Edit Envelope window, the first instance of the sound appears as a dark gray waveform against a white background. Repetitions of the sound appear as a medium gray waveform against a light gray background. A vertical line marks where one loop ends and the next begins. These vertical lines are good locations to start and stop your effects because they will go in time with the music.

## Making Your Own Loops

Programs such as Sonic Foundry's ACID (for the PC) are ideal for creating your own Flash soundtracks. Because ACID is a loop-based music creation tool, you can combine several instruments to create your own music. ACID automatically matches the key and tempo of individual loops for you. After you create your original tune, you can save smaller portions of it as seamless loops for use in Flash.

# How to Layer Sounds

You learned some important things in the previous task, and they will help you create truly dynamic musical backgrounds for your Flash animations. Here, you'll learn some basic steps that expand the previous technique even further. By placing several compatible audio tracks on individual layers, you can greatly economize on the audio requirements in your Flash movie. Start and stop the instrument layers at will to add variety to your background music, and use the loops to create a song as brief or as long as you need. The audio requirements stay relatively the same, no matter how long the song is. All you need are a series of loops that play in the same key and tempo, and you're off to a great start.

## ➊ Select Your Loops

Select between four and eight loops that play in the same key and tempo. Keep their lengths at 32 beats or less. Here, the bass track, drum track, and four synth tracks will play at different points in the song. Add guitar, piano, or horn solos for fillers.

## ➋ Add the Loops to the Library

Select **File**, **Import to Library**. Locate the loops you want to use in your movie. Select them all, and select **Open** to import them into your library.

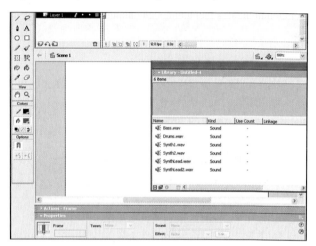

## ➌ Create a Sound Folder

Click the **Insert Layer Folder** icon to insert a layer folder into the Timeline. Name the folder **Music Track**.

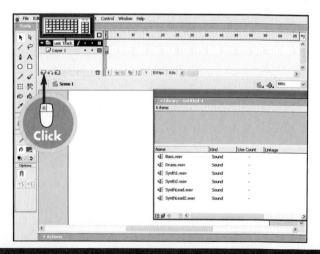

## 4  Edit the First Layer

Rename Layer 1 to a name that applies to one of your tracks. Then add a keyframe (**F5**) to match the length of your movie, or to match the length of the music you want to create. Switch to the Tiny view of the Timeline to view more frames if necessary.

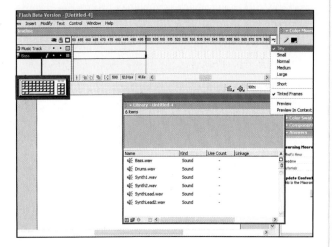

## 5  Add Additional Layers

Add a layer for each of the additional sounds that you imported and name them accordingly. The additional loops automatically contain the same number of frames as the previous layer. Then drag and drop the layers into the Music Track folder.

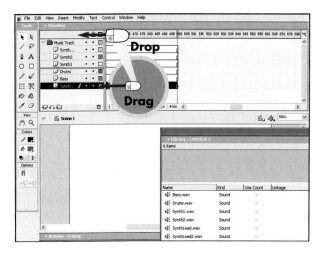

## 6  Add the Sounds

Drag each sound from the library and place it into its appropriate layer. Remember to select the appropriate layer in the Timeline first, and then drag and drop the sound onto the Stage.

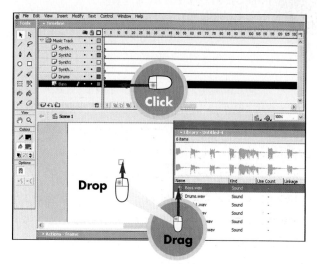

## 7  Loop the Sounds

Open the **Properties** window, and loop each sound for the same number of times (as described earlier in Task 5, "How to Loop Sounds"). Set the sounds to Stream sync while you develop your score so that you can stop playback as necessary. Remember, though, to change all the tracks to Event sound before you publish your movie.

## 8 About Volumes

Depending on your mixture of loops, you might hear distortions when you play more than one at a time. This occurs when the same instruments play in more than one loop. Plan your mix on a diagram if necessary, coloring in the measures in which a sound plays. In this example, only one synth loop plays at a time. You can also adjust layer volumes to achieve the right balance. The following steps show you how.

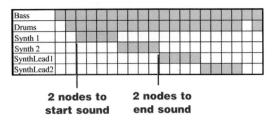

## 9 Plan Your Song

You are limited to eight nodes per sound track, but you can use them to mix your song. In this example, the song starts with a bass solo in the first measure, followed by the drums in the second. The synth tracks alternate throughout the song for variance.

2 nodes to start sound    2 nodes to end sound

## 10 Start a Song

In the Edit Envelope window, a vertical line shows where loops start and end, and you can increase or decrease your volumes at these points. To start your song with a single instrument, simply turn "off" the other sounds by adding nodes that set the beginning volume of each to 0. Keep them off until you want the sounds to begin.

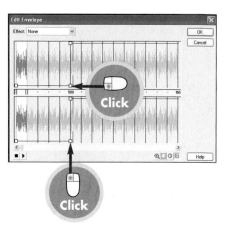

## 11 Adjust Volume and Panning

To adjust volumes, increase or decrease the volume nodes in both channels. To fade, add nodes that go from maximum to no volume or from no volume to maximum. To pan, increase the volume of one channel above the center line and reduce the other channel by the same amount below the center line.

**Left Channel Fades In**     **Pan Left to Right**

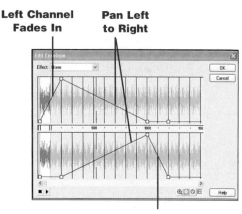

**Right Channel Fades Out**

## ⑫ Turn On and Off Sounds

When you turn on or off a sound, make sure that the change is abrupt—that is, make sure that the "on" and "off" nodes occur at the same point in time. You'll notice that when you move the nodes left or right, they automatically snap to the loops' start/end points. Use this to your advantage.

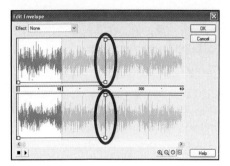

## ⑬ Before You Publish

Before you publish your file, change all the sound layers to Event sound. If you keep it at Stream, the file size increases proportionally to the length of the movie, which doesn't really save you anything. However, if you use the Event sync option, the overhead for the music loops stays at about the same amount in the project, no matter what the length of the movie is. That is the beauty of this approach.

How to Hint

## Why This Way?

You might be wondering why you repeat each loop through the entire song and use volumes to turn on and off each sound. There are two reasons—first, you want the timing to stay perfect, and introducing a sound later might throw it off. Second, you don't want your music to pause later when it has to download a new sound. It's best to load them all in at the beginning and adjust the tracks as necessary.

## Selecting Loops Wisely

A good length to start with is 8–32 beats of music. You can get away with 8 beats of a drum or bass track (why use 32?), but you might need to use 16 or 32 beats of the main files so as not to sound too repetitive. You also might want to keep drums, bass, and lead instruments on tracks of their own so as not to run into the volume problems discussed in step 8.

# How to Sync Sound and Animation

In general, adding sound effects to an existing animation is much easier than creating animations in time with the sound. Often, when you create the animation first, keyframes already exist where significant events occur, and they help you determine where to add sounds. Simply create sound layers and place keyframes in the appropriate locations to start and end your sounds.

## ① To Sync Sound with Animation

Create the animation to which you want to add sound effects. We'll use the (quite common) example of a bouncing ball.

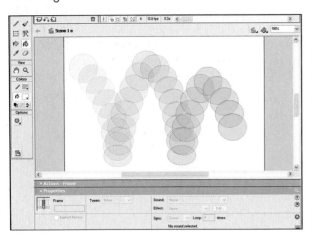

## ② Observe Where Keyframes Lie

Chances are good that you'll have keyframes in some of the frames that require a sound effect (for example, a thud when the ball hits the ground). The animation keyframes help you determine where you need to insert keyframes for your sound effects.

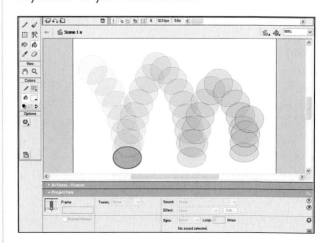

## ③ Create a Sound Folder and Layers

Create a sound layer for each sound effect you intend to add. If you need multiple sound effects, you can create a Sounds folder and place several sound layers in the folder.

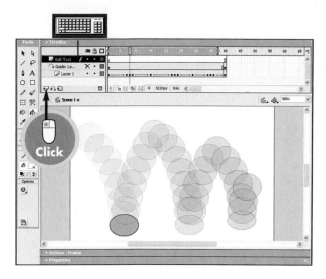

## ④ Create Keyframes

In this example, a layer is created to add a sound effect when the ball hits the ground. Press **F6** to add a keyframe where you want the sound effect to start. Here, a keyframe appears at each frame in which the ball hits the ground.

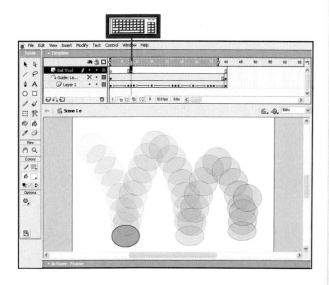

## ⑤ Add the Sound

Add the desired sound to each keyframe you added in the previous step, and select the Synchronization option that best fits the situation (refer to Task 1, "How to Import Sounds and Add Them to a Movie," and Task 2, "How to Choose a Synchronization Option"). For example, a brief Event sync sound is the best option to use here when the ball hits the ground.

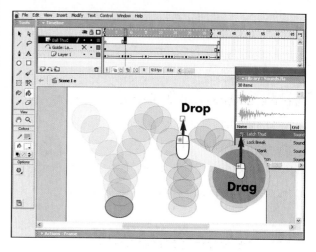

## ⑥ When Animation Keyframes Don't Exist

Suppose you create a tween that causes a plane to enter the Stage from the left side and fly off Stage at the right. Keyframes appear only at the start and end of the tween. You want the motor sound to fade in as the plane approaches the Stage, pan left to right while the plane is on Stage, and fade out as it moves away.

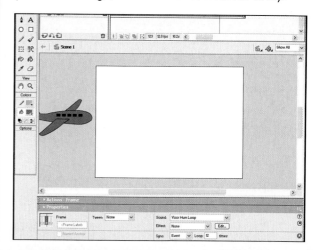

## ⑦ Add the Sound

Find a motor sound that plays seamlessly when it loops. Create a sound layer for the motor sound, and add a keyframe in the same frame in which the airplane tween starts. Loop the sound as many times as it takes to equal or exceed the length of the airplane tween.

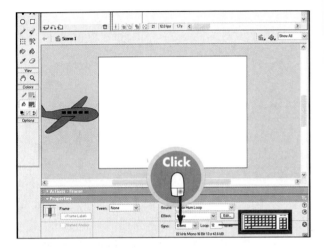

## ⑧ Determine Sound Requirements

Use the frame indicator to scrub through the Timeline until you find the frames in which the airplane enters and leaves the Stage. In this example, it enters at frame 21 and leaves at frame 121.

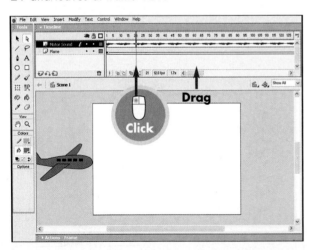

## ⑨ Review Sound Requirements

Open the **Edit Envelope** dialog box. Using the effect shown in Task 6, step 11, create a fade-in for the motor sound in the first segment (frames 1–21), pan from left to right at full volume while the airplane is on Stage in the second segment (frames 22–120), and create a fade-out in the third segment as it flies away (frames 121 until the end).

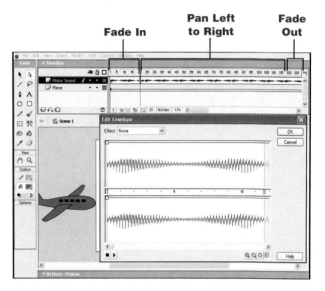

## ⑩ Add a Fade-In

Click the **Frames** icon to display the frame numbers in the Edit Envelope window. Add a node at frame 21. Then adjust the volume of the left channel (the top channel) to 0 at the beginning, and adjust the right channel (on the bottom) to 0 volume in the first segment.

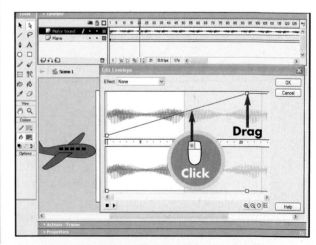

## 11  Add the Pan

To create the pan, add a node at frame 121. Set the left channel (the top channel) to minimum level and the right channel to maximum. Then, at the frame in which the plane leaves the Stage, reverse the volumes (right channel at maximum and left channel at 0). The sound will pan from left to right when you play it.

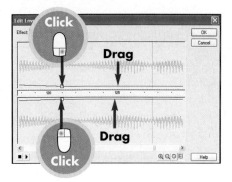

## 12  Add the Fade-Out

Because the left channel is already at minimum volume, all you need to do now is add a node at the end of the right channel to bring the volume down to 0. Now your sound effect is complete.

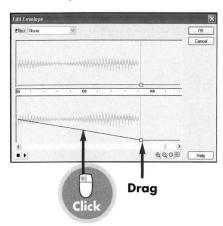

## 13  Test the Movie

To test your movie, select **Control**, **Play** or press **(Return) [Enter]**. You'll hear the sound increase in the left channel until the plane comes to the screen. Then it will pan from left to right and fade out as the plane flies away.

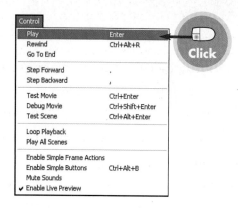

### How to Hint

## Animating to Music

What if you want to go the other way and create an animation that plays in time with music? Use a metronome or a basic drum track (such as a solid bass drum beat) as a visual guide to when the beats occur, or start and end your timing when a loop repeats.

## Calculating the Number of Frames per Beat

To calculate the number of frames in one beat of a song, multiply the frames per second of your movie by 60 and divide that by the number of beats per minute of the song. For example

10fps × 60 = 600 / 120bpm = 5 frames per beat

# Creating a Sniffer

When users navigate to your Web site, it's good practice to check whether they have the Flash plug-in installed before you direct them to Web pages that contain Flash. If they don't have the Flash plug-in, you can automatically direct them to an alternate home page that does not require the Flash plug-in. You can use a sniffer to accomplish this.

Although many sniffers are written in JavaScript and require a browser that is compatible with that scripting language, you can also use Flash itself to create a basic sniffer. This project shows you how.

### ❶ Create a New Flash Movie

Create a new movie by selecting **File**, **New** or by pressing (⌘-**N**)[**Ctrl+N**].

### ❷ Set the Movie Properties

Select **Modify, Document** (⌘-**J**)[**Ctrl+J**] to open the **Document Properties** dialog box. Set the movie size to 18 by 18 pixels. Select a background color for the movie, if desired. Then click **OK** to exit the **Document Properties** dialog box.

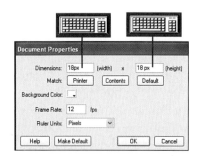

## ③ Add an Action to the First Frame

Right-click the first frame, and select **Actions** from the pop-up menu. The **Actions** panel expands beneath the stage. Expand the **Browser/Network** menu, and double-click **getURL**. In the **URL** field, enter the URL for the Web page that will contain the Flash version of your home page (such as `flashindex.htm`, shown here). Collapse the **Actions** panel.

## ④ Save the Movie

Select **File, Save** (⌘-**S**)[**Ctrl+S**]. Save the movie as `sniffer.fla`.

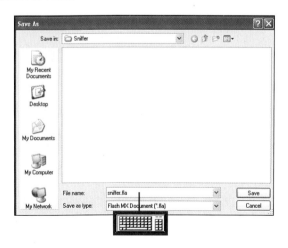

## ⑤ Choose the Flash Formats to Publish

Select **File, Publish Settings**. In the **Formats** tab, use the default selections of **Flash** (.swf) and **HTML** (.html).

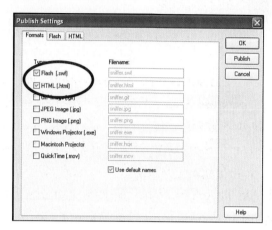

## ⑥ Choose the Flash Settings

Click the **Flash** tab of the **Publish Settings** dialog box. From the **Version** drop-down menu, select the latest Flash version you want to support. (Remember that if you choose an earlier version of Flash, none of the movies on your site can use a later version or contain any features that were introduced in a later version.)

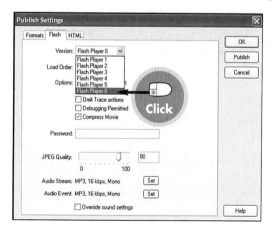

## ⑦ Choose the HTML Settings

Click the **HTML** tab of the **Publish Settings** dialog box. From the **Template** drop-down list, select **Flash Only**. All the other settings can use the default values, as shown here.

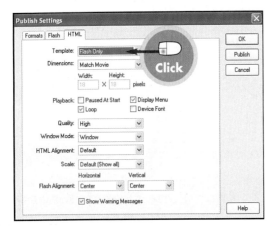

## ⑧ Publish the SWF File

Click the **Publish** button in the **Publish Settings** dialog box; then click **OK** to exit the dialog box. Flash saves the SWF file in the same folder to which you saved the FLA file in step 4. By default, Flash names the file sniffer.swf.

## ⑨ Rename the HTML File

Navigate to the folder that contains your published movie. Rename the sniffer.html file index.html (or whatever the default home page is named on your Web site).

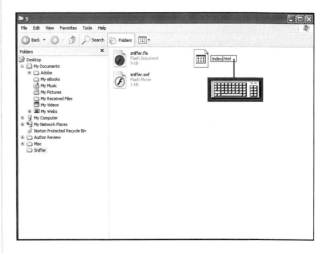

## ⑩ Edit the HTML File

Open index.html in a text editor or Web page editor, and add the following META tag immediately after the <TITLE> tag. The content number indicates the number of seconds that pass before the page refreshes. The URL corresponds with the version of your home page that appears when users do not have the Flash plug-in:

```
<META http-equiv="refresh" content="10"
URL="noflashindex.html">
```

## ⑪ Place the Files on Your Web Site

Locate the default home page (as named in step 9), the sniffer movie (as named in step 8), the Flash home page (as named in step 3), and the non-Flash home page (as named in step 10) in the root folder of your Web directory. You can locate the files in other folders on your Web, if desired, but you will need to edit the URL paths accordingly in the steps indicated.

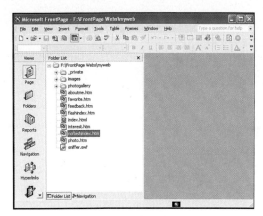

## ⑫ Test the Sniffer

To test the sniffer, first browse to the `index.html` page with a computer that does have the Flash plug-in. The sniffer should direct you to the `flashindex.html` page (or the home page with the Flash movie). Next, browse to the `index.html` page with a browser that does not have the Flash plug-in. The sniffer should direct you to the `noflashindex.html` page (or the home page that does not contain the Flash movie) as shown here.

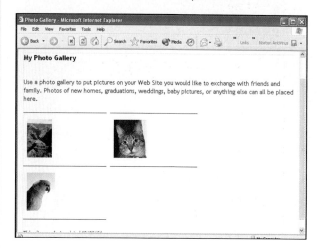

Task

# Saving and Publishing Files

**7**

You've learned a lot about Flash throughout this book, but you're not quite done. You still need to learn how to deliver your project. Although Flash provides several ways that you can deliver your movies, this part focuses on preparing your Flash movie for distribution on the Internet.

The Flash Player format (.swf) is the main format used to display Flash movies in Web pages or with the standalone player. It supports all the functionality of a Flash movie and keeps file sizes manageable. The **File, Publish** command creates the Flash Player file and writes the proper HTML code required to play your movie on a Web page. To view the Flash movie, users must add a special plug-in to their browsers. The Flash plug-in is freely available from Macromedia's Web site.

You can also distribute standalone Flash Player movies, more commonly known as *projector files*. Projector files are standalone executable files that do not require a browser, making them ideal for distribution on disk or CD.

# How to Test Movie Download Performance

The users who connect to your site do so at varying speeds—dial-up modems, DSL, cable, T1, T3, and so on. When you save your Flash movie, you want it to perform well for the majority of your users. After you determine the slowest connection speed that is common to your users, you can test your Flash movie to see how it performs at that speed. This task walks you through a test of the download performance of your movie.

## 1 Test a Scene or the Entire Movie

To test the current scene in a movie, select **Control, Test Scene**. To test the entire movie, select **Control, Test Movie**. The test environment opens and the movie or scene begins to play.

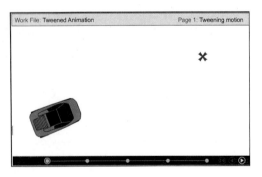

## 2 Choose a Download Speed to Test

Select a download speed from the **Debug** menu. Determine the connection speeds your target audience is likely to use. Select a preset speed from the list, or select **Customize** to define your own settings. The movie stops playing when you select a new speed during playback.

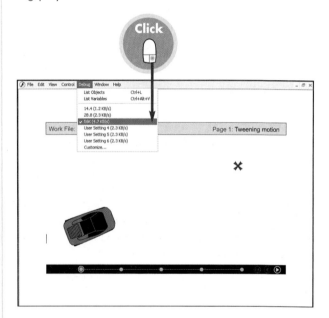

How to Hint

## Opening Existing Shockwave Files

After the **Bandwidth Profiler** is open, you can evaluate any existing SWF file with it. Select **File, Open** and navigate to the SWF file you want to test.

## 3 View the Bandwidth Profiler

Select **View, Bandwidth Profiler** (⌘-**B**) [**Ctrl+B**] to toggle on and off this option. When you click the bars in the graph, details for the selected frame appear in the left section of the profiler. If the bars go above the red line in the graph, your movie will pause while information downloads from the Web server. The goal is to keep the frames at or below this point wherever possible.

Frame details       Bandwidth profiler

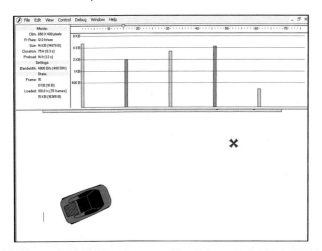

## 4 Set View Options

You can view the Bandwidth Profiler graph in two modes. Select **View, Streaming Graph** or use the keyboard shortcut (⌘-**G**) [**Ctrl+G**] to simulate bandwidth. Select **View, Frame by Frame Graph** or use the keyboard shortcut (⌘-**F**) [**Ctrl+F**] to view the bandwidth required for each frame.

## 5 Show Streaming

Select **View, Show Streaming**. A green progress bar grows from left to right across the Timeline. This simulates the amount of the file that is downloaded to the local machine. Playback begins after enough information is downloaded. If the Playback Head catches up to the streaming bar, the movie pauses while more information downloads.

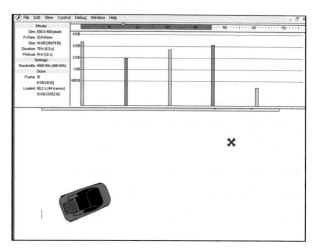

## 6 End the Performance Test

After you run your tests and note the problem areas, select **File, Close** or click the **Close** box to end the performance test and exit the test window. The main Flash editing window appears.

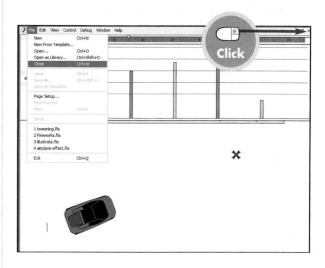

# How to Choose Your Publishing Formats

The first step in the publishing process is to select the file formats you want to publish. The following task briefly describes the many ways you can publish your Flash movies. You select these formats from the **Publish Settings** dialog box.

## ❶ Open the Publish Settings Dialog Box

Select **File, Publish Settings** to open the **Publish Settings** dialog box.

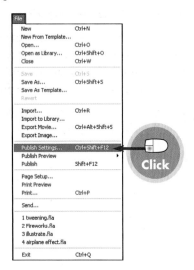

## ❷ Publish a Flash Movie

Notice that the **Flash (.swf)** and **HTML (.html)** options are checked by default. When you publish a movie with both of these options checked, Flash automatically generates a Web page that displays your movie in a Web browser, based on the settings you select in the **Flash** and **HTML** tabs. You'll learn more about these tabs in Tasks 3 and 4.

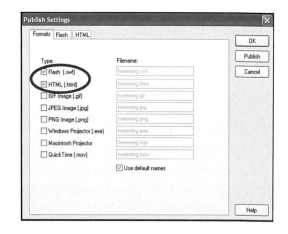

## ③ HTML Settings

Use the **HTML** tab to select the HTML tags and attributes Flash generates for the Web page. The properties determine the position, alignment, image quality, playback options, page dimensions, and more. You'll learn more about these in Task 4.

## ④ Publish Bitmap Files

You can also publish the first frame of your movie as a GIF, JPG, or PNG bitmap image that can be viewed in any Web browser. If your Flash movie contains buttons, Flash generates code to designate the buttons as clickable "hotspots" in an imagemap. These hotspots enable the user to navigate to other pages in your Web site. Bitmap images are perfect for creating static versions of Flash navigation bars.

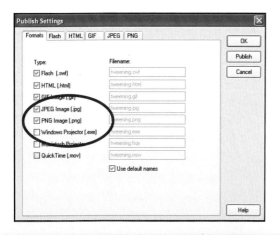

## ⑤ Publish Projector Files

Projector files are self-contained Flash movies that use an EXE (Windows) or HQX (Mac) extension. Projector files can be viewed outside a Web browser and are excellent for presentations and other instances when a Web browser is not required for viewing. You'll learn more about how to choose projector settings in Task 5.

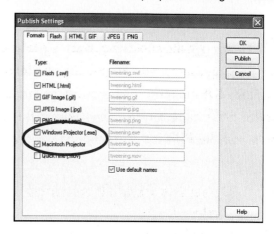

## ⑥ QuickTime Movies

Flash also enables you to publish your Flash movies so that they are compatible with another popular streaming media format: QuickTime. Consult your user manual for further information about this format.

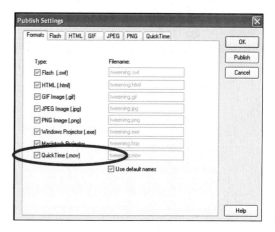

# How to Select Flash Publishing Options

The **Flash** tab in the **Publish Settings** dialog box helps you configure the publishing settings for Flash SWF movies. The options in this tab control the loading order of the layers in your movie, whether others can debug or edit your movie, access to sound settings, and which version of Flash is the highest supported version.

## 1 Choose a Load Order

Use the **Load Order** drop-down list to choose the order in which the Flash player loads the layers in your Flash movies. **Bottom Up** loads the layers from bottom to top; **Top Down** loads the layers from top to bottom.

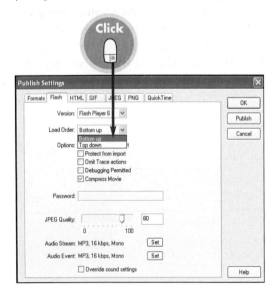

## 2 Choose Options and Password Protection

Check the **Generate Size Report** option to create a report that lists the amount of data in each frame. Check the **Protect from Import** option to prevent other Flash users from importing your Flash movie into their own Flash projects. If you want others to help you remotely debug problems in your movies, check the **Debugging Permitted** option. Enter an optional password for the importing and debugging options.

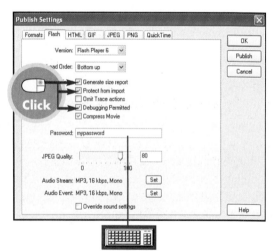

## ③ Set JPEG Quality

Adjust the **JPEG Quality** slider to control the amount of compression used for all bitmaps in your Flash movies. A setting of **100** provides the highest image quality but also makes your Flash movies larger and slower to download. Lower the setting to improve the performance of your Flash movies when it contains bitmaps. You might need to experiment to achieve the right balance between file size and image quality.

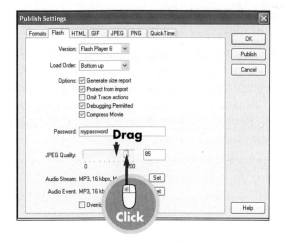

## ④ Specify the Audio Properties

Two settings are provided for audio files. The **Audio Stream** settings control the quality of audio files that use the **Sync** stream setting. Use the **Audio Event** settings to control the audio output quality for sounds with **Event** or **Start** sync settings. These settings are explained in more detail Part 6, "Sounds."

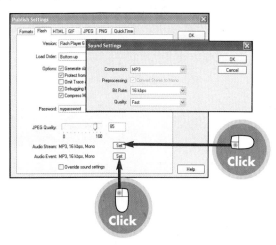

## ⑤ Choose a Flash Version

Flash MX includes many features and enhancements that are not available in previous versions of Flash, including many new ActionScript commands. However, you can also focus your design on features that are compatible with earlier Flash versions. Then, you can select the appropriate version from the **Version** drop-down list when you publish your file.

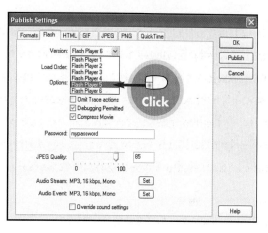

## ⑥ Publish the File

The settings you enter in the **Flash** tab remain in the **Publish Settings** dialog box whether you publish the file or not. To publish the Flash movie with the current settings, click the **Publish** button. Flash publishes the movie to the same folder in which your original Flash project (.fla) is located. Click **OK** to exit the **Publish Settings** dialog box.

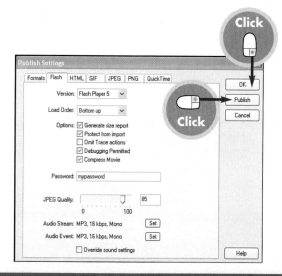

# How to Select HTML Publishing Options

The HTML settings control how Flash generates the HTML Web page that accompanies your Flash movie. When visitors navigate to your site, the Web page serves as a container for your Flash movie. Depending on the options you select here, the HTML code controls the placement, size, and quality of the Flash movie that displays on the page.

## ① Choose a Template

Use the **Template** drop-down menu to select an HTML template from which to generate your Flash HTML page. Click the **Info** button beside the **Template** drop-down menu to read a brief description of each template. Where appropriate, the Info description also includes other publishing options you must choose. For example, if you select **Image Map**, the Info box tells you to select **GIF**, **JPEG**, or **PNG** on the **Formats** tab.

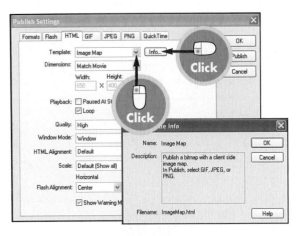

## ② Specify Dimensions

The **Dimensions** drop-down menu enables you to select an option for movie size. Select **Match Movie** to create a Flash movie that displays at the same size as your movie project. If you want to create a movie that is sized differently from your movie project, select either **Pixels** or **Percent** and enter the appropriate dimensions in the **Width** and **Height** fields.

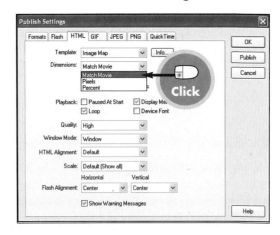

## ③ Choose Playback Options

The **Playback** options control how the user interacts with the movie. Select **Paused at Start** to begin the movie only after the user clicks a button or selects **Play**. Deselect the **Loop** option to play the movie only once, and select the **Display Menu** option to display a shortcut menu when the user right-clicks the Flash movie on your Web page. Check **Device Font** (in Windows only) to substitute fonts that do not reside on the user's system with antialiased system fonts. This option can result in Flash movies that do not appear exactly as you designed them.

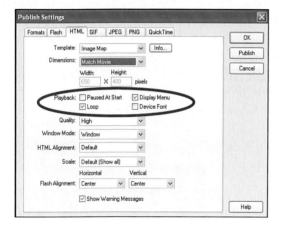

## ④ Select Movie Quality

The **Quality** drop-down menu enables you to choose the quality of your movie. To publish a movie that focuses on playback speed, select **Low** or **Auto Low**. To publish a movie that balances speed and quality, select **Auto High** or **Medium**. To publish a movie that displays at the best quality, select **High** or **Best**.

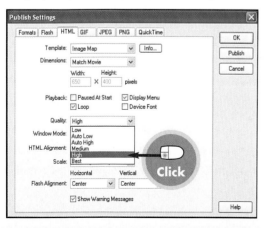

## ⑤ Specify the Window Mode

The **Window Mode** drop-down menu (Windows version only) enables you to select a window mode for your Flash movie. The default, **Window**, displays the Flash movie in its own rectangular window on a Web page. Select **Opaque Windowless** to hide Web page elements behind the Flash movie (in conjunction with Dynamic HTML). Select **Transparent Windowless** to display the Web page background through any transparent areas in your Flash movie. This last option can reduce the playback speed of your movie.

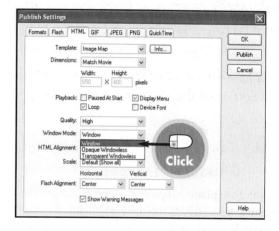

## ⑥ Set Alignment and Scale

The **HTML Alignment** drop-down menu controls the position of the movie on your Web page.

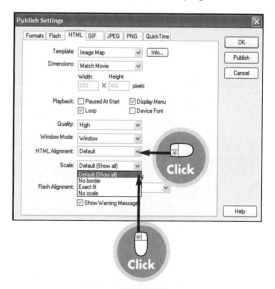

# How to Publish Flash Projectors

**S**ometimes you want to deliver your Flash movie outside of an HTML page (for example, on disk or CD). Flash projectors come to the rescue. Projectors are standalone applications that can be played back on most computers. You can create Windows EXE and Mac HQX projectors. This task shows how to create a projector file.

## ❶ Access the Publish Settings Window

Before you publish, you must specify the publish settings. Select **File, Publish Settings** to open the **Publish Settings** dialog box. It opens to the **Formats** tab.

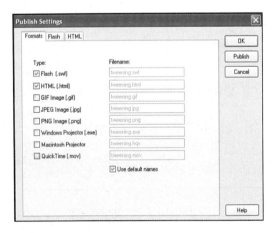

## ❷ Choose the Projector Option

From the **Type** checklist, check the appropriate option for the projector you want to create. Select **Windows Projector (.exe)**, **Macintosh Projector**, or both options.

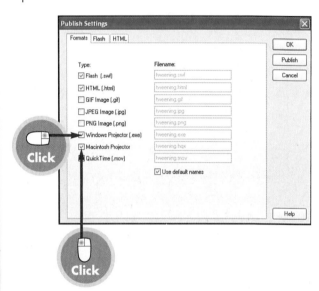

## ③ Name the Projector File

You can accept the default name for the projector or give it a new name. To edit the name fields, click the **Use Default Names** box to uncheck it. Double-click inside the projector filename field to highlight the default name, and enter a new name. Be sure to include the proper file extension (.exe for Windows, .hqx for Mac). Press the **Tab** key to move out of the field.

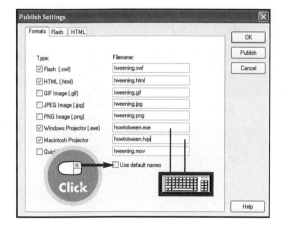

## ④ Publish the Projector File

Click the **Publish** button to create the projector file from the **Publish Settings** window. Flash publishes the file to the same location that holds the original Flash project file.

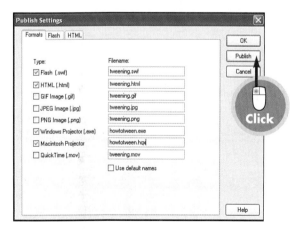

## ⑤ Close the Publish Settings Window

Click the **OK** button to close the **Publish Settings** window.

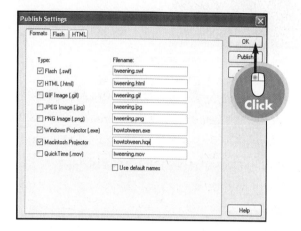

## ⑥ Test the Projector File

Navigate to the new projector file on your computer, and run the file to ensure that it opens and plays properly. See Task 6 for details on playing a projector file.

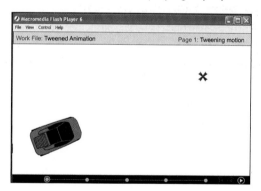

How to Hint

## Publishing to Earlier Versions

When your Flash movie contains features that apply to Flash MX only and if you choose to publish your movie to an earlier Flash version, a warning appears. If this happens, return to the **Flash** tab and select **Flash Player 6** from the **Version** drop-down menu, or edit your movie to remove the features that are incompatible with the version you selected.

# How to Use the Standalone Player

**A** projector file uses a self-contained Flash Player for playback. You can use the Player's commands to control playback of the file. This task explores some of the possibilities.

## 1  Start or Stop Playback

Select **Control, Play** to toggle between playing and stopping the projector.

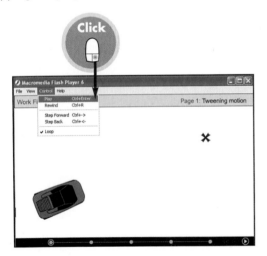

## 2  Navigate Through the Projector

Select **Control, Rewind** to reset the play position to the beginning of the file. **Control**, **Step Forward** and **Control**, **Step Backward** enable you to step through the projector movie in small increments.

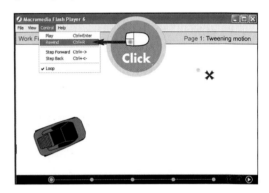

## 3  Loop Playback

Select **Control, Loop** to toggle looped playback mode on and off. When in looped playback mode, the projector plays continuously, starting over from the beginning every time it reaches the end. This continues until you select **Control, Play** to toggle off playback or exit the projector.

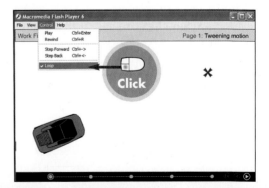

## 4    Adjust the View

**Select View, 100%** to show the artwork at regular size, or select **Show All** to fit the movie in a window of any size. The **Zoom In** and **Zoom Out** options enable you to zoom closer or farther away. Select **View, Full Screen** to resize the projector window to fill the entire computer screen. The **Quality** option enables you to lower or raise the image quality depending on performance needs.

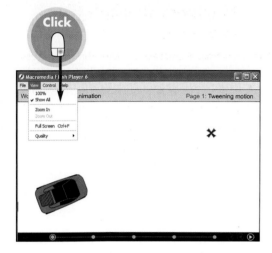

## 5    Access the Context Menu

(Ctrl-click) [Right-click] anywhere in the projector window to access the **Context** menu. Here, you will find most of the same menu options available in the regular menus.

## 6    Exit the Projector

Select **File, Exit** to exit the projector. Alternatively, press the keyboard command (⌘-**Q**) [**Ctrl+Q**], or click the window's **Close** button.

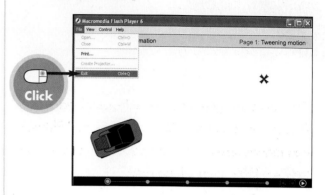

# Appendix A
# Macromedia Flash Resources

Learning Flash is an ongoing process. In this appendix, you will find a listing of Flash resources on the Web. Several online Flash communities offer online tutorials, source .fla files, bulletin boards, news, and links to other sites. You can also find resources for audio, images, and fonts. Additionally, we've included a couple of inspirational sites you might want to visit.

## Tutorials and Communities

### Flash Kit

http://www.flashkit.com

This site offers downloadable tutorials so that you can see the .fla source files as well as click through the tutorials. It offers sounds, as well.

### Flashlite

http://www.flashlite.net/

Good source for tutorials and Flash news.

### Flazoom.com

http://www.flazoom.com/

Good source for links to Flash sites and Flash news.

### Macromedia

http://macromedia.com/support/flash/

You can't beat going straight to the source.

### Moock.Org

http://www.moock.org

General resource not only for Flash but for all things Web.

Colin Moock's site is a great resource because it not only makes information on Flash easy to understand, but he puts it in the context of the whole Web. This is the site to check out if you need to find the process to make Flash talk to JavaScript or to find out why your Flash movie isn't showing up even though you've used the embed tag.

### The Flash Academy

http://www.enetserve.com/tutorials/

This site offers intermediate-to-advanced tutorials in the form of Shockwave files. They're easy to click through and follow along with.

### Virtual-FX

http://www.virtual-fx.net/

Tutorials on all levels, from beginner to advanced action scripting, are offered at this site. There also is a library of open source .fla files, articles, and links to other Flash sites.

## Content Sites

### Audio/Sound Sites

#### ACIDplanet.com

http://www.acidplanet.com/

ACID is a loop-based music creation tool made by Sonic Foundry (http://www.sonicfoundry.com). At ACIDplanet.com, you can download a free version of the software (ACID XPress), download free music loops that change frequently, and buy loop collections on CD.

## Music 4 Flash

http://www.soundshopper.com/

This is a good resource that offers free sounds, but it also has some high-end options if you want to pay for them. It's a thorough site so that those who are unfamiliar with the use of sound can get a lot of information. It also has several links to other resources.

## Wavcentral

http://www.wavcentral.com/

This offers wave files and so much more. It's a good place to find sound (WAV only) as well as miscellaneous effects.

## Winamp

http://www.winamp.com/

This one can be tricky, but it offers MP3 files that can be converted to AIFF or WAV files.

# Images/Photos

## Artville

http://creative.gettyimages.com/artville/
Artville

As mentioned before, this can be accessed from GettyOne. It has both illustrations and photos.

## Clip Art

http://www.clip-art.com/

This site offers a variety of bitmap clip art in cartoon style. It also offers tutorials on image optimization as well as free downloads.

## Clip Art Connection

http://www.clipartconnection.com/

This site offers free clip art.

## GettyOne

http://www.gettyone.com/

GettyOne is an umbrella site that offers a host of sites from high-end (expensive) to low-end (cheap) image options. It's a powerful resource, but you can't legally get free images. Images are divided into royalty-free and licensed images. Keep in mind that royalty-free is not actually free; it means you pay only once, as opposed to a licensed image, which you have to pay for every time you use it. Artville and Photodisc are good low-cost options.

## Photodisc

http://photodisc.com

Another site accessible from GettyOne, Photodisc is a searchable site that offers low-cost, low-resolution files.

# Fonts and Miscellaneous

## Emigre

http://www.emigre.com/

Emigre is a great source for fonts. Keep in mind, though, that they're not free.

## GS Homepage

http://nebula.spaceports.com/~huge/

This Web site offers a selection of free fonts.

## T-26

http://www.t26font.com/

This site is a digital type foundry started by Carlos Segura, an internationally known designer who lives in Chicago. It's not free, but the fonts are beyond compare.

# Inspirational Sites

## Communication Arts

http://www.designinteract.com/
Communication Arts

This is a magazine that covers the graphic/ad and design community. The interactive section of its Web site always has a site of the week, and often it's a Flash site.

## Pray Station

http://www.praystation.com

This is a site from a group working out of the MIT Media Lab. Joshua Davis is the mastermind behind this site and many others, such as http://barneys.com. The site is created with Flash and features a number of projects that you can view.

# Glossary

**.fla file**  An editable Flash file.

**.swf file**  A Flash file meant only for distribution—it can be watched, but not edited.

## A

**ActionScript**  The computer language Flash uses for actions.

**Animated graphics**  Moving images of any type. Often, Flash graphics and animated GIFs are image types seen on the Web.

**Aspect ratio**  The ratio of height to width. Similar to a television or movie screen, the shape of a Flash animation remains the same—no matter its size.

## B

**Bitmapped graphic**  *See* Raster graphic.

**Blank keyframe**  A keyframe that causes nothing to appear on Stage. *See also* Keyframe.

**Button**  An item a user can click that causes an action.

**Button state**  A visual version of a button. For example, during clicking, the button is in its Down state; when dormant, it is in its Up state. When the mouse is hovered over the button, the button is in its Over state.

**Button symbol**  A symbol used to create interactive buttons that respond to mouse events. *See also* Symbol.

## C

**Coordinates**  Numbers signifying a place in a Cartesian plane, represented by (x,y). The upper-left pixel in Flash, for instance, is written (0,0) or (0x,0y).

## D

**Down state**  A button state that occurs when the user clicks the button with his mouse.

## E

**Export**  To move a file or object from a Flash file. Often, the term *export* is used to discuss the creation of distributable Flash files.

## F

**Focus**  The state of being active. In Flash, a dark line indicates which option has focus in a Timeline. *See also* Timeline.

**Frame rate**  The rate, stated in frames per second (fps), at which each frame in an animation is played back for the user.

**Frame-by-frame animation**  Animation using a series of keyframes with no tweening that creates a flip-book-like animation Flash file. *See also* Keyframe and Tween.

## G

**Graphic symbol**  Used for static images and to create reusable segments of animation. The animation that appears in a graphic symbol is locked into the same Timeline as the main movie.

**Grid**  Similar to grid paper, a grid is used for precise placement of objects in a Flash file. *See also* Ruler.

**Guide layer**  A special layer that does not export when you export a Flash file. This layer can be used to help registration of various elements of a Flash file.

## H

**Hit state**  The clickable area of a button.

**Hyperlink**  Text or an object (such as an image) that can be clicked to take a user to related information, as used on the World Wide Web.

**Hypertext Markup Language (HTML)**  The language read by Web browsers to present information on the Internet.

## I

**Import**  To bring a file or an object into a Flash file.

**Instance**  An occurrence of a symbol used from the Library—especially helpful because, although more than one instance can exist, only the master symbol must be saved; thus, file sizes are kept small. *See also* Library and Symbol.

**Interface**  The design with which users interact.

## J–K

**Keyframe**  A frame in which you establish exactly what should appear on the Stage at that particular moment in time.

## L

**Layer**  Aptly named, one of a "stack" of media in a Flash file Timeline. This is especially useful in animation because only one object can be tweened per layer. *See also* Tween.

**Library**  A storage facility for all the media elements used in a Flash file.

## M

**Masking**  In Flash, a layer that contains shapes that will display or hide various areas of the stage. To implement the mask, you need at least two layers: one for the Mask and one that is Masked (such as Motion Guide and Guided). The graphical contents of the Mask layer determine which parts of the Masked layer show through. *See also* Motion Guide.

**Morph**  A type of animation that naturally transitions one shape to another. *See also* Shape Tween.

**Motion Guide**  A Guide layer that has an adjacent layer (below it) that is set to Guided. Tweened objects in the Guided layer follow a path in the Guide layer.

**Movie Clip symbol**  Symbols that contain interactive controls, sounds, and even other Movie Clips. Movie Clips can be placed in the Timeline of Button symbols to create animated buttons. Movie Clips follow their own internal Timelines, independent of the main Timeline. *See also* Symbol.

## N–O

**Onion-Skin tools**  Tools that enable you to edit one keyframe while viewing (dimly) as many frames before or after the current frame.

**Over state**  A button state that occurs when the user passes her mouse over a button. *See also* Button state.

## P

**Panning**  An effect that makes a sound seem to move from left to right (or right to left).

**Parameter**  A specifier used in ActionScript. *See also* ActionScript.

## Q

**QuickTime**  A video format created by Apple. A common file format found on the Internet.

## R

**Raster graphic**  An image file format that contains the color information for each pixel. Raster graphics' file sizes are relatively large, unlike a vector graphic. *See also* Vector graphic.

**RealPlayer**   A streaming video player created by Real Networks. RealMedia (RealPlayer files) is a common format on the Internet.

**Registration**   The process of ensuring that things are properly aligned (often from one frame to another). *See also* Guide layer.

**Rollover sound**   A sound effect that plays any time a user places his cursor over a button.

**Ruler**   Similar to a physical ruler for Flash, a ruler is used for precise measurement of objects in a Flash file. *See also* Grid.

**Runtime**   The point at which the user is watching your movie (as well as when you're testing the movie).

## S

**Scale**   To resize as necessary.

**Scene**   A component part of a Timeline in a Flash file. *See also* Timeline.

**Scrub**   A technique to preview your animation by dragging the red current frame marker back and forth in the Timeline.

**Shape Tween**   A utility to create a fluid motion between two objects. *See also* Tween.

**Smart Clip**   A Movie Clip with unique parameters in it that performs certain actions.

**Stage**   The large, white rectangle in the middle of the Flash workspace where a file is created. What is on the Stage is what the users will see when they play your Flash file.

**Statement**   A single line of code in a script. *See also* ActionScript.

**Static graphics**   Graphics with no animation or interactivity. The computer-image equivalent of a photograph or painting.

**Symbol**   Although any object in a library is technically a symbol, symbols mainly refer to a Graphic, Movie Clip, or Button that is stored in the Library. This is especially useful because no matter how many instances of a symbol are used, it must download only once, and changes made to the master symbol are immediately reflected in all instances already used. *See also* Button symbol, Graphic symbol, Library, and Movie Clip symbol.

**Sync**   The timing between an animation and a corresponding sound. You choose sync settings in the Sound panel.

## T

**Tile effect**   A raster graphic used as the "fill" color in any shape you draw.

**Timeline**   Object on the Flash workspace that contains the sequence of frames, layers, and scenes comprising an animation.

**Tween**   Used as a verb, "to tween" is to have something be done between two things. For example, you can use a Shape Tween to morph a solid circle into a doughnut.

## U

**Up state**   Normally a button's default state, this occurs when the user has not clicked or passed over the button with her mouse. *See also* Button state.

## V–Z

**Vector graphic**   A vector graphic file contains all the math to redraw the image onscreen (unlike a Raster graphic). A vector graphic's file size remains small, and the image can be scaled to any size without any degradation to image quality. Flash .swf files are saved as vector graphics. *See also* Raster graphic.

# Index

## A

creating, 122-123
email, sending, 129
Go to buttons, 130
   *navigating frames, 130*
   *navigating scenes, 130-131*
Play buttons, 130-131
sounds, adding to, 150-151
Stop button, 131
testing, 136-137
text-only buttons, creating, 123

**calculating number of frames per beat, 167**

**centering Timelines, 104**

**changing**
background colors (movies), 10-11
character spacing, 40
colors, 33
cursors (Pen tool), 27
fills
   *Arrow tool, 47*
   *Paint Bucket tool, 32-33*
guide colors, 12-14
instance brightness, 72
instance colors, 72
instance tint, 73
instance transparency, 73
linear gradient fills, 35
movie dimensions, 181
outlines, 33
radial gradient fills, 35
ruler units, 13
stroke properties, 47
text width, 43
Timeline Frame Views, 81

**character spacing, changing, 40**

**choosing**
button behaviors, 122
download speeds, 174
fill colors, 28
Gap Size, 32
load order (movies), 178
stroke color, 16

**circles, creating, 18**

**clearing**
guides from Stage, 14
keyframes, 83

**Click Accuracy settings, 15**

**Clip Art Connection Web site, 188**

**Clip Art Web site, 188**

**Clipboard, moving text, 45**

**closed paths, completing, 23**

**closed shapes, completing, 23**

**Color Mixer, 7, 10, 29**

**color tweens, creating, 88**
selecting new instance color, 89
selecting tint, 89

**colors**
animating, 88-89
changing, 33
instance colors, changing, 72
multiple effects, creating, 90
selecting, 6-7

**Colors palette**
fills, turning off color, 17
strokes
   *choosing colors, 16*
   *turning off colors, 17*

**Colors panel**
colors, selecting, 7
custom colors, creating, 7
fills, turning off color, 17
strokes, turning off color, 17

**columns, resizing, 65**

**commands**
Add Swatch command, 7
Copy, 45
Copy and Paste commands, 49
Cut, 45
Import, 48
Import to Library command, 49
Optimize, 37
Paste, 45
Smooth, 36
Straighten, 36

**Communication Arts Web site, 188**

# D

fills

   *applying copied fills, 34*
   *applying copied strokes, 35*
   *copying, 34*
   dropshadowed text, creating, 45

**duplicating**

   scenes, 113
   symbols, 71

## E

**email, sending, 129**

**Edit Envelope Dialog Box, loops, viewing, 159**

**editing**

   ActionScripts, 129
   bitmaps, 55
      *with image editing programs, 54*
   directional fade (sound), 153
   lines, 24-25
   looped sounds, 155-157
      *adding effects, 158*
      *silent segments, 158-159*
      *zooming in/out of waveform, 158*
   movie clips, 56
   multiple frames, 105
   sound effects, 152
      *directional fades, 153*
      *stereo channels, 153*
   stereo channels, 153
   symbols, 68-69
   text, 44-45

**effects (sound)**

   adding to looped sounds, 158
   customizing, 153
   editing, 152
      *directional fades, 153*
      *stereo channels, 153*
   stereo channels, adjusting, 154

**embedded fonts, 41**

**embedding movie files, 56**

**Emigre Web site, 188**

**enabling/disabling**

   auto kerning, 41
   Lock Fill modifier, 33

**encoding ratio, setting, 57**

**enlarging fills, 35**

**erasing**

   lines, 25
   strokes, 53

**Event Sync, 149**

**exiting**

   Flash, 4-5
   symbol editing mode, 63

**expanding/collapsing libraries, 67**

**Eyedropper tool, 32.** *See Also* **Dropper tool**

## F

**fade-ins, creating, 91**

**fade-outs**

   creating, 90-91
   testing, 91

**file compression settings, testing, 55**

**file size**

   antialiased images, 55
   bitmaps, 49

**files**

   bitmap files
      *importing, 48-49*
      *publishing, 177*
   compressing, 55
   Flash projector files
      *naming, 183*
      *publishing, 183*
   projector files
      *publishing, 177*
      *testing, 183*

**Fill Transform tool, 32**

   linear gradient fills, changing, 35
   radial gradient fills, changing, 35

**filling shapes with bitmaps, 50-51**

**fills**

   applying copied fills, Dropper tool, 34
   bitmap, 53
   bitmap fills, selecting, 29
   changing
      *Arrow tool, 47*
      *Paint Bucket tool, 32-33*
   colors
      *choosing, 28*
      *turning off, 17*

# N-O

# P

# W-Z